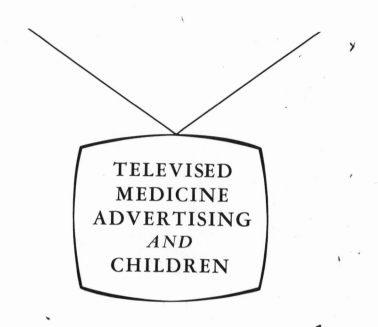

TELEVISED
MEDICINE
ADVERTISING
AND
CHILDREN

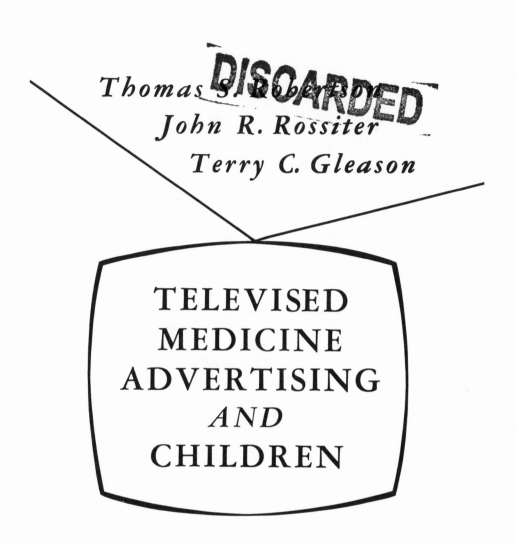

Thomas S. Robertson
John R. Rossiter
Terry C. Gleason

TELEVISED MEDICINE ADVERTISING *AND* CHILDREN

PRAEGER

PRAEGER SPECIAL STUDIES • PRAEGER SCIENTIFIC

Library of Congress Cataloging in Publication Data

Robertson, Thomas S
    Televised medicine advertising and children.

    Bibliography: p.
    Includes index.
    1. Advertising--Drug trade--United States.
2. Television advertising and children--United States.
I. Rossiter, John R., joint author. II. Gleason,
Terry C., joint author. III. Title.
HF6161.D7R6   659.14'3   79-4280
ISBN 0-03-049161-4

This material is based upon research supported by the National Science Foundation under Grant No. APR 76-21130.

Any opinions, findings, and conclusions or recommendations expressed in this publication are those of the author(s) and do not necessarily reflect the views of the National Science Foundation.

PRAEGER PUBLISHERS,
PRAEGER SPECIAL STUDIES
383 Madison Avenue, New York, N.Y. 10017, U.S.A.

Published in the United States of America in 1979
by Praeger Publishers,
A Division of Holt, Rinehart and Winston, CBS, Inc.

9   038   987654321

ACKNOWLEDGMENTS

The authors are indebted to the National Science Foundation for support and to Charles Brownstein for his assistance as NSF program director. This research benefited considerably from the involvement at an early stage of Pradeep Kakkar. The conduct of the research was with the assistance of Linda Applestein, Lee Caudill, Susan Davis, David Gorsline, Frank Hayson, and Elizabeth Jones.

CONTENTS

LIST OF TABLES

LIST OF FIGURES AND EXHIBITS

TELEVISED
MEDICINE
ADVERTISING
AND
CHILDREN

1

OVERVIEW

This book describes the results of an empirical research project specifically designed to assess the effects of televised medicine advertising on children. The sample comprises 673 children between the ages of 8 and 13 years old and their parents. The sample composition includes boys and girls and spans a socioeconomic range from disadvantaged to upper-middle class.

The project objective is to provide an analysis of the relationship between proprietary medicine advertising and children's beliefs, attitudes, and behavior toward proprietary medicines. The effect of proprietary medicine advertising on children is an issue of some currency, yet there is an almost total lack of available empirical evidence on which to base social policy decisions.

The conclusions from this study can be summarized as follows:

Exposure. Children are exposed to proprietary medicine commercials despite the fact that such commercials are neither directed to them nor permitted during children's programs. The average child in the study was exposed to 718 proprietary medicine commercials on an annual basis.

Overall effects. Children's beliefs, attitudes, and requests for medicines are affected by the televised advertising of proprietary medicine products. The effect of advertising is to offset slightly a significant overall decline in children's beliefs, attitudes, and requests for proprietary medicines as children grow older. These offsetting effects are significant statistically, although they are not of a substantial magnitude. First-order correlations (controlling for grade) between medicine advertising exposure and beliefs, attitudes, and requests are from .12 to .22. Incremental explained variance for the medicine advertising exposure variable

1

is from .01 to .03, although advertising works in conjunction with other variables in achieving total explained variance.

Magnitude of effects. The magnitude of effects due to the advertising of proprietary medicines to children is not dissimilar to other advertising research results involving adults. Advertising is obviously a contributory factor in consumption behavior, and an explained variance on the order of 2 percent is common. This may, of course, translate into sizable consumer expenditures. Thus, children are not unreasonably affected by the advertising of proprietary medicines, although one could argue that the effects are considerable given that such advertising was not directed at them in the first place.

Behavioral effects. The relationship between the advertising of proprietary medicines and children's usage of medicines is quite limited, reflecting parental control over medicine intake. However, the relationship does reach a higher significance level among seventh graders, as these children are allowed to self-administer medicines to a limited extent. Perhaps a more appropriate behavioral outcome in assessing medicine advertising's effects on children is requests and, as discussed, there is a significant (although moderate) relationship between advertising and requests.

Subgroup analyses. Children who are highly anxious about illness show heightened (although still moderate) effects of televised medicine advertising. As such, they can be considered a "vulnerable" subgroup within the total set of children. Analysis among young children, disadvantaged children, and children who are frequently ill fails to indicate any consistent pattern of greater susceptibility to persuasion due to televised medicine advertising.

Parental mediation. Parental mediation is found to be somewhat limited as measured by frequency of discussion about illness and medicine. The effect of parental mediation is to lead to more positive child beliefs and attitudes toward proprietary medicines. It may be inferred that such discussions, rather than building discrimination, lead to a greater salience of medicines and it may be that parents find it necessary to provide positive information about medicines in order to encourage intake under illness conditions.

Parent-child independence. The development of children's beliefs and attitudes toward proprietary medicines seems to occur relatively independently of parental beliefs and attitudes. Analysis within the family shows a lack of parent-child correspondence, suggesting that children develop their attitudes based on independent processing of environmental and experiential stimuli. The study, therefore, supports an "independence" model of attitude formation rather than a "correspondence" model and attributes only limited influence to parents just as only limited influence has been attributed to advertising.

Hierarchy of effects. Results suggest the existence of a "hierarchy of effects" leading to requests as the key behavioral variable. There exists a beliefs-attitude-intent-requests sequence such that each step is predicted mainly from the preceding step.

Overall summary. This study suggests that televised medicine advertising performs only a limited role in the formation of children's beliefs and attitudes toward medicines. In the short run, it produces a modest increase in beliefs and attitudes. In the long run, this increase is overshadowed by a significant decline in children's attitudes and beliefs as a function of age and thus cognitive development and experience. The study further indicates a lack of relationship between advertising and usage (which is controlled by parents) and finds no support that children abuse proprietary medicines. Usage levels are moderate and the extent to which parents allow children to self-administer medicines is relatively low.

2

THE RESEARCH CONTEXT

This chapter examines the actual incidence of medicine advertising to which children are exposed. Also, the issues involved in the debate over children and medicine advertising are sketched and the points of view and perspectives of the several parties involved in the debate are outlined.

CHILDREN'S EXPOSURE TO
MEDICINE COMMERCIALS

Because some 85 percent of children's viewing is nonchildren's programs (Adler et al. 1977), it follows that children are exposed to proprietary medicine advertising even though such advertising is not directly aimed at them. Robert Choate (1975), in testimony before the Joint Federal Trade Commission/Federal Communications Commission Hearings on Over-the-Counter Drug Advertising, estimates that children see over 1,000 medicine commercials annually. Earle Barcus (1976), in a 1973 content analysis of television advertising, finds that proprietary medicine advertising accounts for about 6 percent of total product advertising, or an average of one medicine commercial every 57 minutes. The highest frequency is during nighttime hours when there is one medicine commercial every 37 minutes.

In the research described in this report, it was found that the average child is exposed to 718 proprietary medicine commercials per year. This figure was determined by matching the child's reported monthly program viewing with Broadcast Advertisers' Reports*

---

*Broadcast Advertisers' Reports is a syndicated tracking service that tabulates the incidence of television commercials by category for particular geographic markets.

data, which list actual commercials by program for the Philadelphia metropolitan area under study. These data were then extrapolated to the annual estimate of 718 medicine commercials.

Thus, despite industry self-regulation codes prohibiting medicine advertising to children,* children do see sizable numbers of
medicine commercials. Self-regulation codes apply only to programs "designed primarily for children." The National Association of Broadcasters code (1976), for example, defines children's
programming time as "those hours, other than prime time, in which
programs initially designed primarily for children under 12 years of
age are scheduled." This definition, in effect, limits children's
programs to programs shown on weekend mornings and to a limited
number of other programs oriented specifically toward children,
such as "Captain Kangaroo." The guidelines do not apply to most
afternoon programs or to prime time, and these are, of course,
periods of substantial child viewing.

The categories of medicine advertising to which children
might be exposed at approximately the time of the study are indicated in Table 2.1. The leading advertisers of proprietary medicines are shown in Table 2.2.

THE ISSUES

The issues regarding children's exposure to proprietary medicine commercials have come into clearer focus within the past
three years. The impetus for much of the debate can be traced to
the 1975 petition of the attorneys general of 14 states before the
Federal Communications Commission and the Federal Trade Commission requesting a ban on medicine advertising on television between 6:00 a.m. and 9:00 p.m. Although the petition was rejected
on the grounds (primarily) of insufficient evidence for the alleged

---

*The National Association of Broadcasters Advertising Guide-
lines for Children's TV Advertising (1976) specify that: "Nonprescription medications and supplemental vitamin products, re-
gardless of how taken or administered, shall not be advertised in
or adjacent to programs initially designed primarily for children
under 12 years of age" (Item L). Similar provisions exist in the
Children's Advertising Guidelines of the National Advertising Division of the Council of Better Business Bureaus (NAD, 1975): "Medications, drugs and supplemental vitamins (liquid or pills) should
not be advertised to children" (p. 7).

TABLE 2.1

Annual Advertising Levels for Proprietary Medicines

	Spot Advertising	Network Advertising	Total Budget	Count of Network Commercials
Headache remedies, sedatives, and sleeping products	$22,438,700	$73,480,300	$95,919,000	7,191
Cough, cold, and sinus remedies	19,853,600	62,158,200	82,011,800	6,183
Digestive aids	12,614,400	30,527,700	43,142,100	2,290
Laxatives	2,074,200	12,781,200	14,855,400	2,444
Vitamin preparations and tonics	4,674,300	24,176,900	28,851,200	2,530
Medicated skin products and liniments	9,928,100	30,521,000	40,449,100	3,640

Source: Robert B. Choate, "Before the FTC/FCC OTC Drug Advertising to Children Panel," May 21, 1976 (Washington, D.C.: Council on Children, Media and Merchandising).

TABLE 2.2

Most Heavily Advertised Proprietary
Medicine Brands

Brands	Television Annual Expenditures
1. Anacin	$18,685,300
2. Bufferin	9,953,000
3. Geritol Tablets	9,932,900
4. Excedrin	9,680,700
5. Dristan	8,448,300
6. Bayer	8,168,600
7. Alka-Seltzer	7,157,400
8. Contac	6,921,400
9. Di-Gel	6,673,800
10. Sominex	5,316,100
11. Pepto-Bismol	5,220,600
12. Rolaids	5,023,200
13. One-a-Day Vitamin	4,616,900
14. Datril	4,076,300
15. Vicks Nyquil	3,859,200
16. Alka-Seltzer Gold	3,783,700
17. Hold 4 Hour Cough Drops	3,724,800
18. Geritol Liquid	3,568,300
19. Primatene Mist	3,412,700
20. Tums	2,518,700
21. A.R.M. Allergy Relief Medicine	2,115,700
22. Unicap Vitamins	1,715,400
23. Flintstones	1,270,800
24. Femiron Tablets	1,093,100

Note: Based on 1975 network television annual advertising expenditures.

Source: Jack Ryan, "Ad Expenditures for Health and Beauty Aids," Product Management, July 1976, pp. 27-34.

harmful effects, the petition generated a considerable outpouring of issues, concerns, and position statements by its supporters and opponents.

The thrust of the attorneys general petition (1975) was the argument that children are "particularly impressionable and susceptible to the influence of television" (p. 8) and that medicine commercials aim to create "receptive attitudes toward pill taking" (p. 16) and to "present drugs as the cure-all to the tension and problems of everyday life" (p. 15). The petition advocated that medicine advertising should be restricted "to an audience which is equipped to evaluate and digest sophisticated drug advertising" (p. 4).

The effects suggested by the attorneys general are basically threefold: that medicine commercial viewing by children encourages excessive reliance on pills, that there may be a relationship between medicine advertising and accidental poisonings, and that such advertising may relate to longer term use of illicit drugs. A brief review of each of these issues follows.

Excessive Reliance on Pills

The concern underlying this issue is that children exposed to medicine commercials may develop an undue receptivity to medicines. Choate (1975), on behalf of the Council on Children, Media and Merchandising, asserts that children who are "repeatedly exposed to O-T-C drug advertising—where adult role models are 'rewarded' for taking medication—are likely to learn a behavioral response from such ads and to act on that learned behavior at some future time—perhaps to their detriment" (p. 19). Furthermore, Choate alleges that advertising builds an association of a "pain pill with a pleasure syndrome that makes everything go away. . . . Madison Avenue, over the airways encourages everyone, including children, to take drugs to get up, to stay awake, to stay slim, healthy and attractive, to eliminate minor pain or discomfort, and to go to sleep" (p. 395).

The Proprietary Association, a nonprofit trade association of proprietary medicine manufacturers, in response to such assertions, points to the lack of available evidence to support them. In its comments to the FCC (1975), the association also elaborated the value of proprietary medicine advertising: "Self-medication is an accepted and essential element in the scheme of health care in this nation" (p. 14) and it is the consumer who must judge "whether or not the symptoms are sufficiently discomforting to warrant the use of self-medication" (p. 14). In addition, "while it is true that young children do not possess the requisite experience and judgment to properly evaluate O-T-C medicine advertising or to make judicious use of the products themselves, this same statement could be made of any advertising not specifically directed to children" (p. 18).

Essentially, there is a lack of empirical evidence to support the arguments advanced concerning a link between advertising and children's receptivity to drugs. However, children are exposed to medicine advertising that, in the words of the Proprietary Association, they do not have the "requisite experience and judgment to properly evaluate." Nevertheless, is this grounds for removal of such advertising from television? Would its removal be adverse to the public interest, if indeed "this advertising serves a legitimate and valuable purpose by informing viewers of both the nature of various symptoms and the availability of products to treat symptoms" (Federal Communications Commission 1976)?

Accidental Poisoning

This is a rather specific issue, but it will be reviewed briefly. It is sometimes alleged that TV medicine advertising creates a favorable aura surrounding medicines. Associated with this depiction is the fear that young children may be intrigued by pill taking and may be tempted to consume medicines kept in the house. Accidental poisoning may occur when children raid the aspirin or cold tablet container or mistake vitamins for candy. The seriousness of poisoning resulting from proprietary medicine consumption is exemplified by the fact that medications are the leading substance accidentally ingested by children under 5 years of age (Action for Children's Television 1975).

Nevertheless, the scope of these problems should be questioned. Admittedly, aspirin remains the single poisoning substance most frequently ingested by children; however, it continues "to decline both absolutely and as a percentage of total ingestions by the under 5 age group" (National Clearinghouse 1974). Moreover, figures cited on medicinal poisoning usually pertain to children under 5 years old, whereas the criticism leveled against television advertising involves 5- to 12-year-olds. For under 5-year-olds, the real issue would seem to center more upon safety caps for bottles and on parental supervision rather than on television viewing habits. Furthermore, there appears to be no evidence linking accidental ingestion of poisons and television advertising.

Illicit Drug Usage

Associated with the fear that medicine advertising may lead to a pill-popping society is the concern that such receptivity to pills will open the door to illicit drug usage. One of the major assumptions underlying the 1975 petition by Francis X. Bellotti, attorney general of the Commonwealth of Massachusetts (and 13 other attorneys general) urging the FCC to "ban all drug advertisements between 6 a.m. and 9 p.m." was this hypothesized OTC*/illicit drug relationship. Francis Bellotti, for example, quoted former Federal Communications Commissioner Thomas J. Houser as follows: "America's drug companies are referred to as becoming our Nation's most formidable drug pushers" (Bellotti 1975, p. 405).

The American Pharmaceutical Association (1972), in testimony before the National Commission on Marihuana and Drug Abuse, reflects a similar position. It asserts that "advertising of drugs is, indeed, contributing in a significant way to the problem of drug abuse" (p. 2). Further, it reasons that: "Bombarding the young mind with the 'pill-for-every-ill' philosophy is reaping its grim harvest as these children grow into adolescence and begin seeking their kicks in their own drug world" (p. 5).

The Proprietary Association (1975), in response to the illicit drug issue, cited a report by Oxtoby-Smith, Inc. (1974) that it commissioned. This review of the literature found no relationship between proprietary medicine advertising and drug abuse. This is consistent with the findings of research by James Hulbert (1974) and Ronald Milavsky and co-workers (1975-76). Indeed, Milavsky, in research with teenagers, finds a slight negative relationship between exposure to proprietary medicine advertising and usage of illicit drugs. This may be explainable if teenagers who are involved with illicit drugs are less home-oriented and therefore see less television. However, exposure to proprietary medicine advertising during teenage years does not necessarily relate to prior exposure patterns, hence it is still possible that heavy viewing among preteens correlates later with illicit drug use as they become teenagers. Choate (1976), for example, after hearing this evidence reflected that ". . . most of the studies showed what teenagers thought about ads seen while they were teenagers; their possible use of illicit drugs obviously was teenage oriented. There was no research on how O-T-C drug ads exposed to sub-teenagers affect teenage drug attitudes. No research at all" (p. 1).

---

*The term OTC, referring to over-the-counter drugs or medicines, is for present purposes synonymous with the term proprietary medicines.

Despite evidence suggesting the lack of a relationship between medicine advertising and illicit drug attitudes and behavior, therefore, some doubt lingers.

THE PARTIES INVOLVED

The social and political context regarding televised medicine advertising is complex. In synopsis, however, there are three principal parties to the debate: public interest groups, private industry, and the federal government.

Public Interest Groups

Concern over the susceptibility of children to television advertising has brought together concerned groups of physicians, parents, teachers, and others desiring to take positive measures "to make TV a creative and constructive force and to eliminate misleading and unfair commercials" (Charren 1975). Two of the more vocal groups to date have been Action for Children's Television (ACT) and the Council on Children, Media, and Merchandising (CCMM). These groups employ a variety of techniques to focus attention upon their cause, including testimony at government hearings, publications, conferences, research sponsorship, and the filing of petitions with regulatory commissions and courts.

These public interest groups view television advertising directed at children as creating a potentially damaging environment for the following reasons:

Advertising may unduly persuade or manipulate the cognitively unsophisticated child	because	Intellectually immature children may be unaware of advertising's persuasive intent; therefore, they may be inadequately prepared to cope with advertising messages.
Advertising may damage the parent-child relationship	because	Parents often cannot or are not willing to respond favorably to the child's requests for products seen on television. This may lead to conflict and resentment.
Advertising may imbue undesirable values, for example, "the need to take pills"	because	The child who watches large amounts of television becomes dependent to a greater extent on television as a source of reality and values.

Private Industry

Medicine manufacturers, advertising agencies, and broadcasters constitute this group. Each has a specific role to conduct in the advertising process: manufacturers develop and market the products; agencies are relied upon by the former to develop creative strategies to help sell these products; and broadcasters sell advertising on locally and nationally shown programs.

In acknowledgment of children as a special interest group, and because the airways are a public resource, the National Association of Broadcasters* has adopted standards for children's advertising as set forth in its Children's Television Advertising Guidelines (1976). These guidelines, as noted, include the banning of televised drug and vitamin commercials directed to children.

The self-regulatory measures promulgated by advertisers and agencies are overseen by the Council of Better Business Bureaus, Inc. In turn, the National Advertising Division (NAD) of the Council of Better Business Bureaus is concerned with the monitoring of commercials and serves as a liaison between advertisers and consumers. In the spring of 1974, a Children's Advertising Unit was established and specifically charged with the responsibility of developing "Advisory opinions on issues involved in this complex matter (of children's advertising), such as safety, social habits, nutrition, hazardous products, and fairness of advertising techniques" (NAD 1976, p. 2). In June 1975, the Children's Advertising Review Unit issued a set of "Children's Advertising Guidelines" with the stated purpose "to ensure that advertising directed to children is truthful, accurate, and fair to children's perceptions." The provisions of the NAD guidelines are similar, although not identical, to the NAD code.

Private industry believes that moral persuasion and self-regulatory measures are sufficient to keep advertising in the public interest. Moreover, industry spokespersons propose that the critics of TV advertising have ignored the following benefits:

Advertising prepares the child for his or her role as an active consumer	because	Television advertising informs the child as to product availability and choice and encourages the child to consider what the various items can offer.

---

*Approximately 60 percent of commercial stations are members of NAB, including a majority of the larger stations.

Advertising enhances the parent-child relationship	because	Television advertising fosters discussion between the parent and child regarding products advertised.
Advertising merely reinforces existing beliefs	because	Television advertising is a secondary influence when compared with the socializing potency of parents and peers.

The Federal Government

This group primarily consists of two main government agencies, the Federal Trade Commission (FTC) and the Federal Communications Commission (FCC), authorized by congressional legislation to regulate broadcast advertising. The FTC is responsible for the regulation of the content of commercial messages and the FCC is concerned with the amount and scheduling of advertising. Both commissions perform quasi-judicial (hold hearings) and quasi-legislative (make rules) functions.

The FTC and FCC recently have begun to assume a more active role in helping to define the parameters of television advertising with respect to children. To this end, the FCC has established a Children's Television Task Force to investigate the impact of television advertising on children.* In December 1976 the FCC rejected the attorneys general petition to reduce the television time periods available for medicine advertising. The basis for this rejection was that: "Empirical evidence to support the claim of a causal connection between misuse or abuse of drugs and televised advertisements of over-the-counter drugs" was missing (FCC 1976). Furthermore, the commission questioned its constitutional authority to enact the action proposed by the petition.†

---

*Under the supervision of Karen S. Hartenberger, director of the FCC's Children's Television Task Force, two days (May 20-21, 1976) of panel discussions at the FCC were held to "explore the possible impact of televised over-the-counter drug advertisements on children, adolescents and adults."

†"Neither Section 326 of the Communications Act (47 U.S.C. 326) nor the First Amendment of the Constitution enfranchise this licensing agency (FCC) to ban categorically a narrow class of speech which has not lost its legal protection." See Broadcast Action: "Joint Concurring Statement of Commissioners Hooks and Washburn on Bellotti Petition," News Report, no. 14754, Federal Communications Commission, Washington, D.C., December 14, 1976.

The Food and Drug Administration (FDA) of the Department of Health, Education, and Welfare is also (indirectly) involved in the television advertising issue because of the FTC proposed OTC medicine rule requiring that advertising claims be consistent with FDA-approved label claims. An FDA advisory panel is presently studying nonprescription pain killers, and although the FDA holds no official authority regarding the advertising of OTC medicines, it can advise both the FTC and FCC.

Government agencies face considerable difficulty in attempting to assess the environment created by TV advertising, for the following reasons:

Government's actions regarding advertising receive widespread attention	because	The FTC and FCC are empowered with legislative authority; therefore, their decisions have far-reaching implications.
The government is uncertain as to what actions to take concerning TV advertising	because	Solid empirical evidence has been inadequate and relatively scarce.
The government is concerned with the legitimacy of taking action on advertising	because	Action against advertising may be in violation of the First Amendment and the "no censorship" provision of the Communications Act.

SUMMARY

The effects of proprietary medicine advertising on children is an issue of some currency. Yet there is an almost total lack of empirical evidence on which to base social policy decisions concerning medicine advertising and children. Children are exposed to some 718 medicine commercials annually, but the impact of this exposure is not known. In the present project the focus is on proprietary medicine's effects on children between 8 years old (third grade) and 12 or 13 years old (seventh grade). The study is not concerned with younger children or with teenagers. Furthermore, it is not concerned with illicit drugs. The project's objective is to provide a definitive analysis of the relationship between proprietary medicine advertising and children's beliefs, attitudes, requests, and usage of proprietary medicines.

Action for Children's Television. 1975. "Before the Federal Trade Commission, A Petition to Promulgate a Rule Prohibiting the Advertising of Vitamins on Children's and Family Television Programs." Washington, D.C., October.

Adler, Richard P., et al. 1977. Research on the Effects of Television Advertising on Children. Washington, D.C.: U.S. Government Printing Office.

American Pharmaceutical Association. 1972. "Statement to the National Commission on Marihuana and Drug Abuse." Washington, D.C., July 17.

Attorneys General. 1975. "Petition of the Attorneys General to Promulgate a Rule Restricting the Advertising of Over-the-Counter Drugs." Before the Federal Trade Commission, Washington, D.C., August.

Barcus, G. Earle. 1976. "Over-the-Counter and Proprietary Drug Advertising on Television." In Communication Research and Drug Education, edited by Ronald E. Ostman, vol. 3, pp. 89-111. Beverly Hills, Calif.: Sage Publications.

Bellotti, Francis X. 1975. "Statement Before the Subcommittee on Communications, Hearings of the Committee on Interstate and Foreign Commerce." House of Representatives, July, Serial No. 94-53.

Charren, Peggy. 1975. "Statement, Hearings Before the Subcommittee on Communications of the Committee on Interstate and Foreign Commerce." House of Representatives, July 14-17, p. 23.

Choate, Robert B. 1976. "Before the FTC/FCC OTC Drug Advertising to Children Panel." Washington, D.C.: Council on Children, Media and Merchandising, May 21.

_____. 1975. "Petition of the Council on Children, Media and Merchandising to Issue a Trade Regulation Rule Governing the Private Regulation of Children's Television Advertising." Washington, D.C.: Federal Trade Commission, March.

Federal Communications Commission. 1976. "Request for Ban on Television Drug Ads Denied." News Report, no. 14747, December 10.

Hulbert, James. 1974. "Applying Buyer Behavior Analysis to Social Problems: The Case of Drug Use." In Proceedings of the American Marketing Association, edited by Ronald C. Curhan, pp. 289-92.

Milavsky, J. Ronald, Berton Pekowsky, and Horst Stipp. 1975-76. "TV Drug Advertising and Proprietary and Illicit Drug Use Among Teenage Boys." Public Opinion Quarterly 39 (Winter): 457-81.

National Association of Broadcasters. 1976. "Advertising Guidelines: Children's TV Advertising." New York, January 1.

National Advertising Division. 1976. "Advertising to Children: Report of a Seminar Conducted by the Children's Advertising Review Unit." New York: Council of Better Business Bureaus, June 18.

_____. 1975. "Children's Advertising Guidelines." New York: Council of Better Business Bureaus, July.

National Clearinghouse for Poison Control Centers. 1974. Tabulations of 1973 Reports. Washington, D.C.: Food and Drug Administration, May-June.

Oxtoby-Smith, Inc. 1974. Why Do American Youth Use Illicit Drugs? Supplement No. 4 to the April 1971 Report. New York.

Proprietary Association. 1975. "Comments in Opposition to the Proposed Rule to Prohibit Advertising of Drugs in Television Before 9:00 p.m." Before the Federal Communications Commission, Washington, D.C., August.

Ryan, Jack. 1976. "Ad Expenditures for Health and Beauty Aids." Product Management, July, pp. 27-34.

3

LITERATURE REVIEW

There is little systematic research evidence on the effects of medicine advertising on children. Most research has focused on teenagers rather than children, and has been concerned with illicit drug use rather than the use of proprietary medicines. Moreover, existing research has generally sought to document the harmful effects of medicine advertising and has ignored potentially beneficial effects.

There is also no useful conceptual framework concerning proprietary medicine advertising and its effects on children. The tendency has been to assume a simple cause-and-effect relationship, although other sources of information and attitudes—parents, peers, siblings, and teachers—obviously work in conjunction with television advertising. The relative effects of these several socializing agents on the child's conceptions of medicine, as well as the contribution of such variables as the child's age, medical history, parent-child interaction style, and family background, are generally not considered as part of existing research paradigms.

With these qualifications in mind, the available, but limited, empirical evidence will be reviewed. First, the literature review begins by delineating what may be considered the major study to date, the NBC study by Ronald Milavsky, Berton Pekowsky, and Horst Stipp (1975-76). Second, a synopsis of another significant study by Charles Atkin (1975) is presented. Last, the review refers to other studies that have examined, if only indirectly, the relationship between televised medicine advertising and children's beliefs, attitudes, and behavior. Table 3.1 presents a comparison of the NBC study, the Atkin study, and the present Wharton study.

TABLE 3.1

A Comparison of the Three Studies

	NBC Study	Atkin Study	Wharton Study
		Design	
Basic methodology	Modified multiwave panel survey	Survey	Survey
Sample	Teenage boys and parents (N varies by wave—822 present for at least one wave); initial random selection balanced by socioeconomic status (SES) but modified by addition of friends and a later subsample which was part of another study	Fifth, sixth, and seventh graders; (N = 256) convenience sample; no parental interviews	Third, fifth, and seventh graders and parents (N = 673); school districts selected by socioeconomic status (SES): random selection of classes by grade
		Variables	
Dependent variables	Intent and usage of illicit drugs and proprietary medicines (represented by two headache medicines, two cold medicines, one stomach medicine, and one sleep medicine)	Beliefs, attitudes, and usage of proprietary medicines (represented by one cold and one stomach medicine)	Beliefs, affect, intent, requests, and usage of proprietary medicines for specified symptoms (headache, cold, cough, stomachache)

18

Exposure to proprietary medicine commercials	Hours of exposure to programs during last four weeks (stratified random sample) multipled by amount of drug advertising on these programs	Limited report on TV viewing of prime time and news multiplied by attention to four medicine commercials	Hours of exposure to programs during last four weeks (stratified random sample) multiplied by amount of drug advertising on these programs
Other variables	Typical variables include age, socioeconomic status (SES), IQ, family structure	Typical variables include age, sex, socioeconomic status (SES), and scholastic performance	Typical variables include age, socioeconomic status (SES), illness experience, illness anxiety, parental medicine mediation and control, and use of medicine information sources

Source: J. Ronald Milavsky, Berton Pekowsky, and Horst Stipp, "TV Drug Advertising and Proprietary and Illicit Drug Use Among Teenage Boys," Public Opinion Quarterly 39 (Winter, 1975–76): 457–81; Charles K. Atkin, "The Effects of Television Advertising on Children: Survey of Pre-Adolescent's Responses to Television Commercials," A report submitted to Office of Child Development, Department of Health, Education, and Welfare, 1975; and present study.

THE NBC STUDY

The most ambitious study to date is the NBC study by Milavsky, Pekowsky, and Stipp (1975-76). This is a modified panel design consisting of five waves of interviews with teenage boys and two waves of interviews with their parents over a period of three and one half years (May 1970 to December 1973). The focus of this study is on illicit drug use, but proprietary medicine use is also included. The strength of the study is its measure of exposure to proprietary medicine advertising based on a rigorous assessment of viewing factored by Broadcast Advertisers Reports (BAR) data that provide actual incidence of proprietary medicine commercials by program. The weakness of this study is its relatively simple conceptual framework (essentially exposure and usage). Some issues also arise as to the sampling process, which is random initially but then adds multiple friends per respondent. The validity of the proprietary medicine usage measure is questionable (in one wave, usage of only five brands of medicines, which would not seem to represent total usage) and the measurement changes from wave to wave. Also, the reliability of the measures is not reported.

The results germane to a concern with proprietary medicines (but recognizing that this is a teenage sample) are as follows:

There is a positive, but relatively weak, relationship between exposure to proprietary advertising and reported use of drugs (a correlation of tau B = .07, p < .05, in one wave and tau C = .12, p < .001 in a later wave using a more extensive usage measure).

This relationship is accentuated (but not significantly) in homes where there are many proprietary medicines around the house but does not seem to be affected by child-initiated versus mother-initiated dispensing of the medicines.

THE ATKIN STUDY

The Atkin study (1975) employs a broader set of measures than the NBC study. However, it is limited methodologically by its use of a convenience sample, by the measurement of medicine advertising exposure in a rather questionable manner, * and by other

---

*Atkin constructs a medicine advertising exposure index by multiplying amount of viewing ("a lot, sometimes, almost never")

measurement problems based on one-item or two-item scales with no assessment of reliability. Validity may also be questioned, as the dependent measures are based on only cold and stomach generic remedies that may not represent proprietary medicines in general.

Atkin's results may be summarized in terms of the following advertising exposure relationships, all of which are based on sixth-order partial product-moment correlations—controlling for grade, sex, social class, scholarship, child's frequency of illness, and parents' approval of medicine. All except the last correlation are significant at the .05 level.

Perceptions of reality. As exposure to medicine advertising increases, children perceive that people are more often sick ($r = .14$) and that they more often take medicine (.14).

Illness concern. As exposure to medicine advertising increases, children worry more about getting sick (.14).

Approval of medicine. The relationship between medicine advertising exposure and approval of medicine is .12.

Medicine efficacy. As exposure to medicine advertising increases, children are more likely to report that they feel better after taking medicine (.12).

Medicine usage. There is a general lack of relationship between medicine advertising exposure and medicine usage (.03).

In general, these results suggest that medicine advertising exposure does, to a certain extent, influence the child's conceptions of illness and medicine. These relationships tend to be accentuated (but rarely to a significant extent) among the higher scholastic performance children and among the higher social status children. Atkin does not offer any explanation as to why this might be the case. Other variables, such as age and sex of the child, parental attitudes toward medicine, and the child's frequency of illness, all show inconsistent patterns across the conception measures.

Neither the NBC study nor the Atkin study begins to settle the issue of proprietary medicine advertising's impact on children's medicine conceptions. Although both studies provide major contributions to the literature, they are incomplete conceptually and methodologically. Conceptually, neither study provides an adequate model of how televised medicine advertising affects children. Methodologically, neither study reports on reliability.

---

to 15 programs by degree of self-reported viewing of three medicine commercials. This would not appear to represent actual exposure to televised medicine advertising.

Although the NBC study employed multi-item measures of medicine advertising exposure that are likely to be quite highly reliable, the reliability of the "effects" (for example, usage) measures is unknown. The likelihood of serious unreliability problems is particularly acute in the Atkin study for both exposure and "effects" measures. The consequences of unreliability are generally to produce lower correlations than might have been obtained with reliable measures. Low correlations, however, are ambiguous in the sense that they may be due either to measurement error or to small actual correlations between exposure and the effects variables. Given this ambiguity, the possibility remains that the impact of medicine advertising on children is substantially larger than previously reported.

A further limitation of both studies is that neither included children's requests for medicines as an "effects" variable. Both instead focused on usage. Atkin found a significant zero-order correlation of .17 between advertising exposure and usage and Milavsky et al. found a significant correlation (tau C) of .12 between advertising exposure and proprietary drug use in wave V of their study.

It seems improper to focus on usage as a behavior of the child. More appropriately, the child's usage is a parental behavior, as parents are generally the ones who decide when children should take proprietary medicines. Usage may be an appropriate dependent variable in the Milavsky study with teenagers but, as noted, the study did not relate usage to childhood advertising exposure. In any case, usage is not an appropriate measure of children's responses to medicine advertising.

OTHER RESEARCH

A study similar in concept to Atkin's is that of Charles Lewis and Mary Ann Lewis (1974). A total of 208 children from the fifth and sixth grades, drawn from an experimental school and from a public school serving a disadvantaged population, were asked to watch television and to describe commercials related to health. From the children's reports, the authors inferred that television appears to exert an influence upon health-related beliefs and behavior of children. In particular: personal experience and parental use were found to increase the credibility of the advertising messages, with the lowest level of credibility occurring when neither child nor parent had tried the product; and the frequency of use of advertised products and the frequency of acceptance of the advertising messages as true were highest among children from lower socioeconomic backgrounds. The methodological problems of this study are severe. As the authors themselves note, the two schools viewed television at different times and there was no validation of actual drug usage.

Donald Kanter (1970) found that students in the fifth, seventh, and eleventh grades believed that advertising influences their feelings toward medicine. Many of the students also expressed the belief that other young people were potentially capable of being influenced by proprietary medicine commercials. However, proprietary medicine commercials as a category were not recalled more easily than other commercials and had a low salience to the students (that is, were not talked about much). The youngest children (fifth grade) were the most believing, most receptive, and least critical of medicine commercials, suggesting that it is among younger people that proprietary medicine commercials may have the greatest potential impact. These findings also may indicate that skepticism is a function of age and comes into play more strongly in older children—a finding generally confirmed in research by Scott Ward (1971) and Thomas Robertson and John Rossiter (1974).

John Campbell (1975) investigated the development of concepts of illness among 264 children aged 6 to 12 as a function of their parents' concepts of illness. A developmental trend was evidenced whereby the maturing child's conception of illness began to resemble that held by adults. In sharp contrast, a matching of the conceptions for a particular mother-child pair failed to reveal much consensus of beliefs. This disparity, in Campbell's opinion, attests to the complexity of the transmission process whereby children develop an adult conception of illness. Illness concepts were found to be related to the child's health history as well as age. Furthermore, sophistication of illness concepts was most evident among older children whose health had fared poorly relative to that of their parents.

RESEARCH NEEDS

The question of proprietary medicine advertising's impact on children cannot be definitively addressed with existing research. The problems that the present study seeks to overcome are as follows:

The research to date for the most part has not focused on children but rather on teenagers and college students.

The existing research has generally dealt with illicit drugs and not with proprietary medicines.

There has been no examination of the relative importance and interaction of the various information sources, including media, advertising, parents, peers, and siblings.

Much of the research cited has been coincidental rather than systematically conducted in order to address the issue of proprietary
medicine advertising's impact on children.

Previous studies have tended to use small convenience samples,
have made no attempt to estimate the reliabilities of key variables, and largely have ignored the problem of validating major
variables.

The existing research has not posited a decision process model for
children's medicine behavior. In particular, the dependent
variable has generally been usage, despite the fact that parents,
not children, are for the most part in control of children's use of
proprietary medicines.

The next chapter reviews the research design of the present
study and discusses how many of these problems can be overcome.

REFERENCES

Atkin, Charles K. 1975. "The Effects of Television Advertising on
Children: Survey of Pre-Adolescent's Responses to Television
Commercials." A report submitted to Office of Child Develop-
ment, Department of Health, Education, and Welfare.

Campbell, John D. 1975. "Illness Is a Point of View: The Development of Children's Concepts of Illness." Child Development
46 (March): 92-100.

Kanter, Donald L. 1970. "Pharmaceutical Advertising and Youth."
Coronado, Calif.: Coronado Unified School District.

Lewis, Charles E., and Mary Ann Lewis. 1974. "The Impact of
Television Commercials on Health-Related Beliefs and Behaviors
of Children." Pediatrics 53 (March): 431-35.

Milavsky, J. Ronald, Berton Pekowsky, and Horst Stipp. 1975-76.
"TV Drug Advertising and Proprietary and Illicit Drug Use
Among Teenage Boys." Public Opinion Quarterly 39 (Winter):
457-81.

Robertson, Thomas W., and John R. Rossiter. 1974. "Children
and Commercial Persuasion: An Attribution Theory Analysis."
Journal of Consumer Research 1 (June): 13-20.

Ward, Scott. 1971. "Effects of Television Advertising on Children and Adolescents." In <u>Television and Social Behavior</u>, vol. 4, pp. 432-51. Surgeon General's Report on Television and Social Behavior. National Institute of Mental Health.

4

RESEARCH DESIGN

The objective of the Wharton study is to provide an overall analysis of the relationship between proprietary medicine advertising and children's beliefs, attitudes, and behavior toward proprietary medicines. The study is based on a sample of 673 children and their mothers interviewed during March 1977 in the Philadelphia metropolitan area. Children completed paper and pencil questionnaires in school and mothers (or guardians) were interviewed by telephone within two weeks by professional interviewers from a major national marketing research firm.

RESEARCH QUESTIONS

Overall, the study seeks to determine the relative relationships between proprietary medicine advertising and the following factors: the child's perceived illness level, the child's level of illness anxiety, the child's brand knowledge of proprietary medicines, the child's belief in the efficacy of proprietary medicines, the child's affect toward taking proprietary medicines, the child's intent to take proprietary medicines when ill, the child's medicine request frequency to parents, and the child's usage of proprietary medicines.

Parallel data from parents are also analyzed in order to determine whether child medicine conceptions match parental conceptions. The role of parents as mediators is studied in terms of the importance of parents as an information source concerning medicines, the extent of parental mediation children report, and the degree to which parents control medicine usage. The role of parents is examined as a function of the child's age, social class, and general parent-child interaction style.

VARIABLES

The variables assessed in this study are derived from the relevant literature as reviewed in Chapter 3, as well as the more general literature on the effects of advertising on children (Adler et al. 1977). Additionally, the variables are based on a 1976 pilot study for this project with 439 children and parents, whereby irrelevant variables were eliminated and the data-collection procedures were improved.

The entire set of variables for the study is indicated in Table 4.1. In general, these variables are measured for both the child and the mother. There are a few variables (social class, medicine inventory, medical history, and demographics) where the measure was taken with the parent and then used with the child data. There are also three measures (illness experience, medicine request frequency to parents, and usage of medicines) for which there are both the child's self-report and the parent's report of the child's behavior. The following categorization of variables, although somewhat arbitrary, may help to visualize the scope of the research.

Outcome Variables

These are the dependent variables of interest. The sequence can be thought of in terms of Martin Fishbein's conceptualization (Fishbein and Ajzen 1975). The variables included here are as follows:

Brand Knowledge of Proprietary Medicines

This variable is operationalized (Table 4.1) by matching brand names with symptoms for 12 highly advertised proprietary medicines based on advertising levels for the year preceding the study (Ryan 1976). Parenthetically, note that the use by Ronald Milavsky and co-researchers (1975-76) of brand knowledge as a validity check for their drug exposure index is not particularly compelling because low correlations may stem from advertising's misinforming children by vagueness of indications for use. In an analysis of dental advertisements, for example, Jean Frazier and co-researchers (1974) concluded that 43 percent of the information was inaccurate, misleading, or fallacious.

Beliefs

The beliefs index is keyed to perceived efficacy for the four common medicines deemed relevant to children—cold medicine,

TABLE 4.1

Variables and Measures for Both Children and Parents

Variable	Measurement

Outcome Variables

Brand knowledge of proprietary medicines

Total number of correct responses to 12 questions matching brand names with symptoms, for example, "Contac is":

Aspirin [ ]   Cold Medicine [ ]   Stomach Medicine [ ]   etc.

Belief in efficacy of medicines

Mean of response scores to four symptom-specific questions,[b] for example, "When I have a headache, aspirin can help me feel better" (scored 4, 3, 2, 1).

(Child)   YES [ ]   yes [ ]   no [ ]   NO [ ]

(Parent)   AGREE [ ]   Somewhat Agree [ ]   Somewhat Disagree [ ]   DISAGREE [ ]

Affect toward taking medicines

Mean of response scores to four symptom-specific questions, for example, "When I have a headache, I like to take aspirin."

(Child)   YES [ ]   yes [ ]   no [ ]   NO [ ]

(Parent)   AGREE [ ]   Somewhat Agree [ ]   Somewhat Disagree [ ]   DISAGREE [ ]

Values toward medicines

Mean of response scores to five general value statements, for example, "People take medicines too often."

(Child) YES ☐   yes ☐   no ☐   NO ☐

(Parent) AGREE ☐   Somewhat Agree ☐   Somewhat Disagree ☐   DISAGREE ☐

Intent to take medicines when ill

Mean of response scores to four symptom-specific questions, for example, "When I have a headache, I want to take aspirin" (scored 0, 1, 2, 3).

Never ☐   Sometimes ☐   Most Times ☐   Always ☐

Medicine request frequency to parents[a,c]

Mean of response scores to four symptom-specific questions, for example, "When I have a headache, I ask my parents for aspirin."

Never ☐   Sometimes ☐   Most Times ☐   Always ☐

Usage of medicines[a,c]

Mean of response scores to four symptom-specific questions, for example, "Since school started in September, how many times have your parents given you aspirin?"

0   1   2   3   4   5+ times

Television Factors

Television exposure

Viewing during past week for daily shows and past month for monthly shows of a randomly selected list of 35 shows extrapolated to a monthly basis, excluding shows during school hours and after 11:30 p.m., for example, "How many times did you see "Charlie's Angels" the last four times it was on television?"

0   1   2   3   4

(continued)

Table 4.1, continued

Variable	Measurement
Television coviewing	Report of whether parent viewed each of 35 shows with child at least once during prior four times it was on television.
Medicine commercial exposure	Exposure to medicine commercials derived by combining TV exposure with actual incidence of medicine commercials by program as taken from BAR data (1977) for prior month.
Television control	Mean of response scores to five questions, for example, "Do your parents tell you how late you can stay up to watch TV?" Never ☐ Sometimes ☐ Most Times ☐ Always ☐
Television sets[c]	Number of sets in home and whether child has set in own room.
	Mediation/Parent Factors
Parental medicine mediation	Mean of response scores to five questions, for example, "Since school started in September, how many times have you and your parents talked about medicine commercials that you see on TV?" 0 1 2 3 4 5+ times
Social class[d]	Combined equally weighted measure of occupation and education for head of household.
Demographics[d]	Parents' ages, marital status, education, occupation, religion, number of siblings, and sibling order.

Family interaction style[c]

Schaefer (1977) family interaction scale consisting of 28 items assessing four dimensions: for example, "My parents try to understand how I feel about things."

Yes ☐ No ☐

Medicine control (reverse is child self-administration of medicines)

Mean of response scores to four symptom-specific questions, for example, "Do your parents let you take aspirin without asking them?"

Never ☐ Sometimes ☐ Most Times ☐ Always ☐

Medicine inventory[d]

In-home inventory checklist of 20 highly advertised proprietary medicines.

Illness Factors

Illness experience[a]

Mean of responses to four symptom-specific questions, for example, "How many times a month do you get headaches?"

0 1 2 3 4 5+ times a month

Medical history[d]

Record of child and family's medical history, serious illnesses, injuries, hospitalizations.

Perception of population illness experience

Mean of response scores to four questions estimating incidence of symptoms within the population, for example, "How many times a month do people get headaches?"

0 1 2 3 4 5+ times a month

(continued)

31

Table 4.1, continued

Variable	Measurement
Illness anxiety	Mean of response scores to four symptom-specific and five general questions, for example, "I worry a lot about getting headaches."
(Child)	YES ☐ yes ☐ no ☐ NO ☐
(Parent)	AGREE ☐ Somewhat Agree ☐ Somewhat Disagree ☐ DISAGREE ☐

Other Factors

Variable	Measurement
Information sources	Salience of eight information sources on medicine, for example, "I find out about medicine from (television, doctors, . . .)."
(Child)	YES ☐ yes ☐ no ☐ NO ☐
(Parent)	AGREE ☐ Somewhat Agree ☐ Somewhat Disagree ☐ DISAGREE ☐
Yes/no bias	Series of six questions comprising three pairs of opposites, for example, "I love cats," "I hate cats." Responses were scored in the same direction, regardless of wording. Consequently, respondents with high scores agree with all items.
(Child)	YES ☐ yes ☐ no ☐ NO ☐
(Parent)	AGREE ☐ Somewhat Agree ☐ Somewhat Disagree ☐ DISAGREE ☐

aFor this variable, a measure was also obtained of the parent's assessment of the child's behavior.
bSymptoms were headaches, colds, coughs, stomachaches.
cAsked only of children.
dAsked only of parents.
eThe time frame of some six months was selected after the pilot study indicated relatively low incidence within shorter time periods.

Source: Compiled by the authors.

headache medicine, stomach medicine, and cough medicine (Target Group Index 1975). The focus on efficacy as the central component of medicine beliefs is consistent with Charles Atkin's study (1975). It was felt in the present study that sleeping aids, used in the Milavsky and Atkin studies, were not relevant to children, and this was confirmed in the pilot study.

Affect

In order to test the Fishbein conceptualization, affect is assessed (Table 4.1) across the four common medicines. It has not previously been used in research dealing with medicine advertising effects on children.

Values

An attempt was made to measure general value orientations toward medicines. As noted in the discussion to follow on reliability, this variable does not achieve an acceptable level of reliability and was therefore dropped from the analysis. It appears that the questions asked on values held too many nuances for children.

Intent

The intent variable is necessary to the Fishbein analysis. Basically, it measures the child's readiness to take the four common medicines when ill. A similar "readiness" measure is also part of the Milavsky study.

Requests

This is a critical variable in the study; requests are really the best measure of the child's behavior toward medicines given the low incidence of self-administration. Request behavior is assessed for the four common illness symptoms under study.

Usage

This is the final link in the chain of effects. The measure is based on self-reported usage of the four common medicines for approximately the past six months.

Television Factors

The crux of the study is the role of television advertising of proprietary medicines in determining the child's medicine beliefs, attitudes, and behavior. The variables in the television factors are as follows:

Television Exposure

This measure is a self-report of the child's viewing of 35 randomly selected shows and closely parallels the Milavsky et al. (1975-76) measure.* It was felt that this measure was more valid than the simpler measures of viewing by time period or estimates of hours watched per day as used in some other research. Based on this measure, the child's average weekly viewing of television could be estimated (see Exhibit 4.1).

Television Coviewing

This variable assesses the extent to which parents coview television with children. Coviewing might be expected to modify any exposure/effect relationships.

Medicine Commercial Exposure

This is the study's primary television variable. It is based on the child's television exposure weighted by the actual incidence of medicine commercials for each program as taken from Broadcast Advertisers' Reports data for the Philadelphia market during the survey period. Based on this measure, one can extrapolate to the average number of medicine commercials that a child is exposed to per year.

Television Control

This variable assesses the degree of control exercised by parents in television viewing, for example, programs prohibited or rules on how late the child can watch.

Television Sets

Here the number of sets in the home and whether the child has his or her own set is measured. The expectation is that family-sanctioned individualized viewing may act in an opposite manner to coviewing.

----

*Originally separate measures of the child's viewing of the top ten shows (based on Nielsen data) and the top medicine advertising shows (based on BAR data) were included. These were subsequently dropped in favor of random selection of programs so that a project-able measure of television viewing and medicine advertising exposure would result.

EXHIBIT 4.1

Television Program Selection

Selection of television programs is based on the procedure followed by Milavsky et al. (1975-76). Thirty-five regularly scheduled programs were randomly selected from the time periods sampling those parts of the day when children could be part of the audience:

I	7:00 a.m.-8:30 a.m.	Monday-Friday early morning
II	3:30 p.m.-11:30 p.m	Monday-Friday afternoon and evening
III	7:30 a.m.-11:30 p.m.	Saturday and Sunday all day and evening

The programs selected were broadcast on network and independent stations. Excluded from possible selection were television specials and movies.

The TV exposure index was designed to serve as a general indicator of the respondent's average daily viewing time. Scores on 35 programs were used to calculate a TV exposure index for each respondent. Respondents were asked to record the number of times they viewed the listed weekly and daily television shows out of the last four times they were broadcast. The TV exposure index was derived by multiplying viewing frequency by a program's duration, thereby obtaining its contribution (to the total index score), and summing the contribution of the 35 shows. All shows were extrapolated to a monthly basis.

The following calculations were used in the development of the Wharton study's TV exposure index:

Let f_i = frequency with which show i was watched during last four opportunities

d_i = duration in hours for show i

c_i = contribution to index for show i

Weekly Shows

$$c_i = f_i d_i$$

(continued)

Exhibit 4.1, continued

Most Daily Shows

$$c = 4f_i d_i$$ (Note that this estimates the number of hours watched in a 28-day period reduced by 20 percent. The adjustment reflects the researchers' belief that the reported frequency for the last four shows is likely to be an overestimate of watching behavior.)

"Good Morning America," "Morning News"

$$c_i = 2.5f_i$$ (This reflects the belief that it is unlikely that a child watches the entire show, and that viewing half of the show is more likely.)

"Today Show," "Mike Douglas"

$$c_i = 4f_i$$ (Same as above for one-and-one-half-hour shows)

Three "fake" shows were added to the list of programs in order to provide some check on reporting validity. The frequency distribution of children saying that they watched a fake show is 92.4 percent no incidence, 5.8 percent claimed to watch one fake show, 1.2 percent watched two fake shows, and 0.6 percent watched three fake shows. The fake show measure correlates negatively with grade ($-.21$, $p < .001$), positively with television exposure ($.11$, $p < .005$), and does not correlate with the yes-saying index. The conclusion is that the incidence of fake show viewing is sufficiently low such that overreporting is not a serious problem. Some fake show results are probably due to error by the younger children and, if anything, overreporting would seem to be due to a potential social desirability bias rather than a yes-saying response bias.

Source: Compiled by the authors.

Mediation Factors

The most obvious mediating variables affecting any relationship between television advertising and the child's medicine beliefs,
attitudes, and behavior are parental factors. The variables examined are as follows:

Parental Medicine Mediation

This is an index of parent-child discussion frequency regarding medicines. Such direct mediation would seem to be a logical
variable affecting the child's medicine conceptions and the contribution of medicine advertising to these conceptions.

Social Class

The child's social class background is included, as viewing
levels and mediation patterns may vary by social strata (Adler 1977).

Demographics

Similarly, demographics may influence the mediation process,
perhaps by limiting advertising effects in homes characterized by
higher parental education levels.

Family Interaction Style

This is a general measure of how families interact using
Schaefer's (1977) family interaction scale. The dimensions assessed
are acceptance, acceptance of individuation, rejection, and hostile
detachment. The relationship between family interaction style and
medicine attitudes and behavior will be examined.

Medicine Control

This variable assesses whether parents allow children to take
the four medicine types themselves. The study examines whether
children who can self-administer medicines have different patterns
of beliefs, affect, and usage.

Medicine Inventory

This variable is measured by a checklist of 20 highly advertised proprietary medicines. The question, as raised by Milavsky
et al., is whether availability is associated with increased usage of
medicines.

Illness Factors

A major determinant of medicine beliefs, attitudes, and behavior would logically be the child's illness factors as discussed
below. However, the pattern of cause and effect may not be especially clear. It might, for example, be argued that high exposure
to medicine advertising encourages more frequent feelings of being
ill and in need of medication. Such an effect would be consistent
with adult research that has frequently shown that "illness" is not a
discrete event. A person's definition of self as "ill" seems to depend not only on biological factors but also psychological and socio-
logical factors (Fox 1968).

Illness Experience

The child's report of illness frequency for the four symptoms
is the primary measure of illness experience.

Medical History

Also assessed is the child's more general medical history.
This measure is oriented toward serious illnesses, injuries, and
hospitalizations, and is of less interest given the present focus on
proprietary medicines.

Perception of Population Illness Experience

The expectation here, as suggested by George Gerbner and
Larry Gross (1976), is that heavy viewers of medicine commercials
may systematically overstate the extent of illness among the population. Support for this relationship is found in Atkin (1975).

Illness Anxiety

In line with Barbara Brodie (1974), it was felt that the child's
illness anxiety would affect his or her illness and medicine conceptions. In the 1976 pilot study, Brodie's illness anxiety scale was
used, but because of its questionable reliability (due to the subtlety
of the scale, in the researchers' opinion), another scale was developed and pretested and used in this study.

Other Factors

Finally, two other factors were used in the research.

Information Sources

This is a measure of the salience of eight medicine information sources, including television advertising.

Yes/No Bias

This scale was used to assess the extent of any yes-saying bias.

RELIABILITY ASSESSMENTS

Table 4.2 provides the internal consistency reliabilities for each variable based on coefficient alpha (Cronbach 1951). Internal consistency is the relevant reliability consideration here, as the major indexes are aggregated across symptoms. A number of conclusions are in order:

1. The reliabilities for the children are much better than for parents. It may be that parents make finer discriminations among the four symptoms under study—headache, cold, cough, and stomachache—and have more complex attitude patterns, differentiated by symptom and by the appropriateness of proprietary medicines as a means of treatment than do children.
2. In general, the children's reliabilities are above acceptable levels (.70 or so), except for a few variables.
3. Some variables must be used with caution, however, given low reliability assessments, in particular perception of population illness experience, usage, and television control. The value index was dropped from further consideration due to its low reliability.
4. It is important to note a "positive" lack of reliability on the yes/no bias measure, which indicates the absence of such bias.

SAMPLING

The sample consists of 673 complete mother-child dyads. The children selected are in approximately equal numbers from the third, fifth, and seventh grades. Within each of the grade levels, boys and girls are evenly represented. Ages range between 8 and 13 years old. The sample spans a spectrum of social classes from disadvantaged to upper-middle class. Considerable effort, in fact, was taken to represent adequately children from disadvantaged homes, and they encompass 21 percent of the sample. The approximate social class

TABLE 4.2

Reliabilities[a] of Variables

Variable	Reliabilities		
	Child Measure	Parent Measure	Parental Assessment of Child's Behavior
Outcome variables			
Brand knowledge of proprietary medicines	.67	.51	—
Belief in efficacy of medicines	.81	.59	—
Affect toward taking medicines	.81	.59	—
Values toward medicines	.42	.30	—
Intent to take medicines	.75	.57	—
Medicine request frequency to parents	.76	—	.72
Usage of medicine	.52	.50	.59
Television factors			
Television exposure	.89	.81	—
Television co-viewing	.85	.68	—
Medicine commercial exposure	.73	.51	—
Television control	.54	.58	—
Mediation/parent factors			
Parental medicine mediation	.78	.91	—
Social class	—[c]	.77	—
Family interaction style[b]	.70	—	—
Medicine control by parents	.80	.50	—
Medicine inventory	—	.53	—
Illness factors			
Illness experience	.70	.48	.50
Perception of population illness experience	.59	.69	—
Illness anxiety	.84	.83	—
Other factors			
Information sources	.67	.52	—
Yes/no bias	.07	.26	—

[a]Reliability computed using coefficient alpha.
[b]Average for four dimensions (range is .67 to .74).
[c]Questions not asked of this sample.
Source: Compiled by the authors.

breakdown of the sample (using a combined education and occupation index for head of household) is as follows: disadvantaged 21 percent, working class 34.1 percent, lower-middle class 31.4 percent, and upper-middle class 13.5 percent.

The sample was drawn from six school districts, including the city of Philadelphia and its environs. Each school district provided a selection of schools representing one or more socioeconomic classes, as determined by census tract data (U.S. Bureau of the Census 1972). Twelve schools were selected so as to achieve a distribution of social classes. The majority of schools had all three grade levels available in multiple sections per grade. A random drawing was employed, therefore, to select the specific sections to be included.

The parental sample consists of the mother (or female guardian) of each child who had completed a questionnaire in the previous week. In choosing the mother as the relevant parent, it was felt that she best represented the major caretaker of the child. The demographics of the sample are as follows:

Marital status. Among those interviewed 76.1 percent were married, 8 percent divorced, 8.2 percent separated, 3.4 percent widowed, and 4.3 percent single.

Employment. The percentage of the sample employed was 46.5 percent versus a national average of 42 percent of mothers of school age children (U.S. Department of Labor 1975). Of the employed mothers 56.1 percent held full-time positions.

Education. The educational breakdown of the sample of mothers versus the national average (U.S. Bureau of the Census 1975) is as follows:

	Sample	National
Some high school	16.7%	24.1%
High school graduate	61.0	48.2
Some college	11.8	15.1
College graduate or some graduate school	10.5	12.6

The derivation of the sample is shown in Table 4.3. A total of 1,050 permission letters was distributed to parents, of which 867 were returned. Of the 867 children interviewed, 817 complete files were achieved. Because it was deemed undesirable to have any mother appearing more than once in the data, those instances in which the sampling procedure obtained siblings were handled by randomly choosing only one of the siblings for inclusion in the analysis. Thus,

TABLE 4.3

Derivation of the Sample

Description	Number of Subjects	Percent Reduction	Reasons for Reduction
Number of children's permission letters distributed	1,050	—	
Number of children's questionnaires distributed	867	17.4	Some children were absent from school. Only those children with parental permission slips were allowed to participate.
Number of children's questionnaires completed	817	5.8	Incomplete questionnaires could not be recorded. Reasons for incomplete questionnaires were: Child stopped early; did not wish to continue. Child did not respond to substantial number of questions. Child did not understand the questions due to language difficulties or illiteracy. Child became ill during survey.
Number of parents eligible for interview	795	2.7	Parents were allowed to represent only one child. In 22 cases multiple siblings were interviewed, thus reducing the sample of parents to 795.
Number of parental interviews completed	676	15.0	Reasons for nonresponse were: No telephone listing for parents. No parent/guardian available. Foreign-language problems. Parental refusal to participate. Parental failure to complete entire interview.
Number of child-parent dyads constituting sample	673	0.4	Keypunching errors resulted in three incomplete files.

Source: Compiled by the authors.

the total sample of mothers numbered only 795, of whom 676 were successfully contacted and interviewed. Given some missing data, the end result for analysis is 673 parent-child dyads.

PILOT AND PRETESTS

In 1976 a pilot of this study with 439 children and parents drawn from parochial schools in the Philadelphia metropolitan area was conducted. Results from this study permitted the following:

Eliminate variables. Certain variables, such as peer integration and peer mediation, were found to be of no value in explaining medicine attitudes and behavior and were dropped from the final study.

Add variables. There were certain logical gaps in the pilot study where variables were added, including the medicine requests, brand knowledge, and parent medicine mediation variables.

Reconceptualize variables. Some variables, such as beliefs, were found not to be discriminating and were reconceptualized. In particular, the study moved from general to symptom-specific beliefs and attitudes.

Change measures. A number of measures had poor reliabilities, including the illness anxiety scale and the family interaction scale. This led the researchers to find or develop more reliable measures.

Pretests in three schools and with a limited number of parents were also conducted after the 1976 pilot study in preparation for the final study. The pretests were necessary for the following reasons: (1) to determine whether the individual items and instructions could be understood by the children (particularly third graders). (2) To ascertain whether "disadvantaged" third graders could comprehend and successfully complete the questionnaire. (3) To refine and complete administration procedures for the questionnaire. (4) To see whether any attentional or disciplinary problems would arise with the relatively long administration.

Based on pretest results and observation of the questionnaire administrations, some minor changes to the questionnaire resulted, including eliminating negatively phrased questions that proved confusing to young children; clarifying instructions; and arriving at a common child-oriented language, especially for describing symptoms and medicine categories.

ADMINISTRATION

Children

The questionnaire was administered to the children during the third week of March 1977. In general, children completed the questionnaire in their own classes, although in a few cases the school preferred joint administration to multiple classes in the school auditorium. Teachers were encouraged not to remain in the room, so as to minimize the effects of their presence. The third graders required about 45 to 55 minutes to complete the questionnaire, whereas fifth and seventh graders took only about 35 to 40 minutes.

The administrations were handled by two readers and six proctors who were trained by the Center for Research on Media and Children. Female readers were chosen because it was felt that young children were more often exposed to female adults in the school environment and that females were less threatening in this context than males. The readers' responsibilities were to instruct the children as to what was expected of them (for example, they were assured that this was not a test, simply a personal opinion study); provide the children with examples of answers for the various formats on the questionnaire; and read each item on the questionnaire aloud (as the children followed along in their individual copies). Senior staff members of the center felt that both readers were similar with respect to delivery speed, articulation level, and "comfort" factor for the children.

Each reader was accompanied in the classroom by three proctors. The duties of the proctors were to answer privately questions that a child might have (with standardized replies), to check questionnaires to ensure that no answers were omitted, and to maintain a standardized and orderly administration.

Parents

Parent interviews were conducted during the fourth week of March 1977 by Burke Marketing Research. Administration time averaged 27 minutes per interview. Prior to the administration of the parental interview, the two readers met with staff members of the research company to discuss the instructions and information that was to be related by the interviewers to the parents. Additionally, each item of the interview schedule was read aloud to the staff members to ensure that there were no ambiguities or confusion regarding interpretation. At the commencement of the parental interviewing, the same readers were present in order to answer any questions that might arise and to listen to some of the interviewers. All telephone calls were made from the premises of the research company in a specially designed room equipped with telephone and third-party listening devices.

Throughout the week, random visits were made to the company as a check on the performance of the interviewers and to see if any problems had arisen. The research company assigned a supervisor to oversee the project, that is, to keep in contact with the center regarding the status of the project and to validate calls.

QUESTIONNAIRE

The questionnaires used with children and parents are in the appendix. In general, the questionnaires are the same, except for a few child-only and parent-only questions, as noted earlier in Table 3.1. The scales used for recording responses were altered slightly on some questions so as to be appropriate for delivery over the telephone and so as not to insult parents. Thus, the YES/yes/no/NO format was replaced with AGREE/agree somewhat/disagree somewhat/DISAGREE. The YES/NO format with children was explained in terms of AGREE/DISAGREE. Also, the children's questionnaire was designed and administered in two sections (unlike the parental questionnaire) in order to provide the children with a break.

The children's questionnaire comprises 220 items and the parents' questionnaire 232 items. However, only 181 and 189 items, respectively, are being analyzed. The difference is due mainly to exclusion of items concerning specially selected television programs and to exclusion of vitamins as a type of medicine. In the case of items concerning vitamins, initial analysis strongly suggests that this product is entirely different from the other products in the study. It is rarely perceived as a medicine, and respondents' attitudes and behavior regarding vitamins are inconsistent with those toward other medicines. It appears that vitamins are not a medicine and the responses do not load the same way as with the other products— headache medicine, cold medicine, stomach medicine, and cough medicine. Vitamins, therefore, were taken out of the analysis.

REFERENCES

Adler, Richard P., et al. 1977. Research on the Effects of Television Advertising on Children. Washington, D.C.: U.S. Government Printing Office.

Atkin, Charles K. 1975. "The Effects of Television Advertising on Children: Survey of Pre-Adolescent's Responses to Television Commercials." A report submitted to Office of Child Development, Department of Health, Education, and Welfare.

Broadcast Advertisers Reports, Inc. 1977. "Network TV: Brand Product and Parent Company Schedule Detail and Expenditure Estimates for the Weeks Ending February 20, 27 March 6, 13, 1977." New York: BAR.

Brodie, Barbara. 1974. "Views of Healthy Children Toward Illness." American Journal of Public Health 64, pp. 1156-58.

Cronbach, L. J. 1951. "Coefficient Alpha and the Internal Structure of Tests." Psychometrika 16, pp. 297-334.

Fishbein, Martin, and Icek Ajzen. 1975. Belief, Attitude, Intention and Behavior. Reading, Mass.: Addison-Wesley.

Fox, Renee C. 1968. "Illness." International Encyclopedia of the Social Sciences. Vol. 7, pp. 90-97. New York: Macmillan.

Frazier, Jean P., et al. 1974. "Quality of Information in Mass Media." Journal of Public Health Dentistry 34 (Fall): 244-57.

Gerbner, George, and Larry P. Gross. 1976. "Living with Television: The Violence Profile." Journal of Communication 26, 173-99.

Milavsky, J. Ronald, Berton Pekowsky, and Horst Stipp. 1975-76. "TV Drug Advertising and Proprietary and Illicit Drug Use Among Teenage Boys." Public Opinion Quarterly 39 (Winter): 457-81.

Ryan, Jack. 1976. "1975 Ad Expenditures for Health and Beauty Aids." Product Management, July 1976, pp. 27-34.

Schaefer, Earl S. 1977. "Relationship Inventory for Families." Child Development Center, University of North Carolina.

Target Group Index. 1975. Miscellaneous Drug Products. Report P-20. New York: Axiom Market Research Bureau.

U.S. Bureau of Census. 1975. Current Population Reports. Series
    P-20, no. 276. "Household and Family Characteristics, March
    1974," p. 92. Washington, D.C.: U.S. Government Printing
    Office.

_____. 1972. Population and Housing Census Tracts, Philadelphia,
    1970 Census. Washington, D.C.: U.S. Government Printing
    Office, May.

U.S. Department of Labor. 1975. Special Labor Force Report, 174,
    "Children of Working Mothers." Washington, D.C.: Bureau of
    Labor Statistics.

5

BASELINE RESULTS

In this chapter baseline results for the study are presented. One objective is to sketch an overall profile of children's beliefs, attitudes, and behavior toward proprietary medicines. A second objective is to evaluate the role of parental mediation. A final objective is to assess children's exposure to proprietary medicine advertising and the relationship between exposure and medicine beliefs, attitudes, and behavior.

ILLNESS BEHAVIOR AND CONCEPTIONS

What are children's actual illness levels and conceptions of illness? How do these conceptions vary by age? How do these conceptions differ from parental conceptions?

Children report considerably higher frequencies of illness than parents (coughs, colds, stomachaches, and headaches). The pattern is such that, with increasing age, children's reported illness levels become more similar to parents', although a significant difference remains even at seventh grade between children and parents (see Table 5.1).

Children manifest considerably more anxiety about illness than parents in the sense that they worry more about getting sick. Children perceive higher levels of illness within the general population than do parents. Children also perceive higher population illness than they themselves experience. Although anxiety level and perception of population illness level decline with age, there remains a significant difference between parents and children, even by seventh grade. This anxiety pattern suggests the potential vulnerability of children to mass media stimuli focusing on illness and medicine.

48

TABLE 5.1

Mean Scores on Illness Behavior and Medicine Conception Indexes[a]

Variables	Third-Grade Mean (N = 221)	Fifth-Grade Mean (N = 223)	Seventh-Grade Mean (N = 229)	Parent Mean (N = 673)
Illness behavior and conceptions				
Illness experience[b]	3.1	2.9	2.6	1.5
Perception of population illness incidence[b]	3.2	3.3	3.1	2.6
Anxiety about illness[c]	2.6	2.4	2.2	1.4
Medicine conceptions				
Belief in efficacy of medicines[c]	3.5	3.2	2.9	2.8
Affect toward taking medicines[c]	2.8	2.5	2.4	2.2
Brand knowledge of proprietary medicines[d]	4.0	5.7	6.4	6.8

[a]In general, a between group mean difference of about 0.2 is significant at the .05 level based on Duncan multiple range test, one way ANOVA.

[b]Means based on scale range from 0 to 5, where 5 = high.

[c]Means based on scale range from 1 to 4, where 4 = high.

[d]Means based on scale range from 0 to 12, where 12 = high.

Source: Compiled by the authors.

49

MEDICINE CONCEPTIONS

How much do children believe in the efficacy of medicines and have positive affect toward medicines? How much do children actually know about medicine brands?

Children reflect fairly positive beliefs but rather neutral affect toward medicines. These conceptions change with age such that seventh-grade children are considerably more similar to parents than are third-grade children (Table 5.1 and Figure 5.1). Young children reflect high beliefs in the efficacy of medicines, but "discrimination" increases with age such that the older children have belief levels almost exactly comparable to parents—still favorable, but much less so. The same pattern holds for affect (liking to take medicines when sick), but affect is rather neutral at all age levels.

Actual knowledge of which medicine brands are appropriate to particular symptoms is not very high. Knowledge increases with age such that seventh-grade knowledge level is fairly close to adult knowledge level, but even the adult knowledge level is not particularly good. The extent of correct matching of medicine brands to symptoms indicates confusion about the appropriate use of proprietary medicines, especially as the brand knowledge index was based on brands with large brand shares and high advertising budgets.

MEDICINE BEHAVIOR

To what extent do children request proprietary medicines when ill? What is their reported medicine usage level and to what extent do children self-administer medicines?

Children report considerably higher intent to take medicines when ill and considerably higher actual usage of proprietary medicines than parents (Tables 5.2, 5.3, and Figure 5.2). Usage frequency is generally controlled by parents and self-administration levels are fairly low (Table 5.4). The youngest children request medicines when ill to a greater extent than they receive them but this phenomenon changes such that among fifth and seventh graders, usage of medicines equals or exceeds requests. Once again, these patterns are such that with increasing age, children become more like their parents in intent and medicine usage behavior.

A set of relationships of interest is that between illness experience and intent, requests, and usage. This is shown below by grade level and for parents. In general, the correlations are pronounced and increase with age. The correlations are highest for usage, suggesting that the child's actual illness experience is a dominant factor for parental administration of proprietary medicines.

FIGURE 5.1

Medicine Conceptions

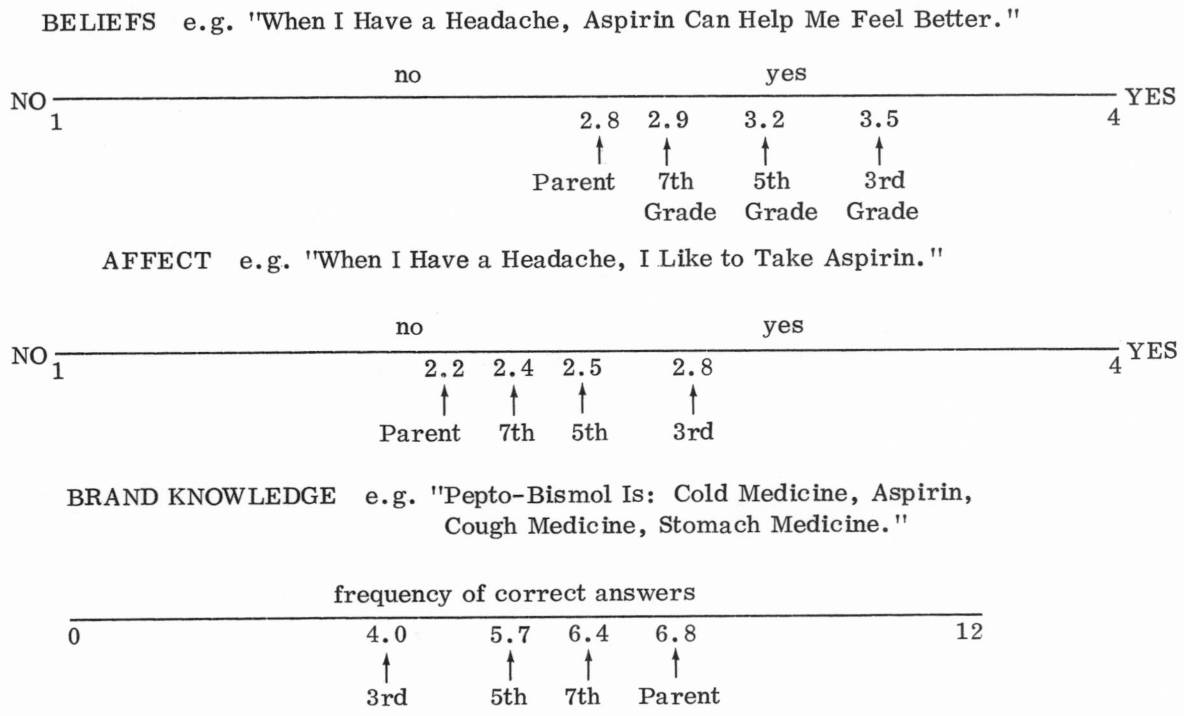

BELIEFS e.g. "When I Have a Headache, Aspirin Can Help Me Feel Better."
no
yes
NO
1
YES
4
2.8
Parent
2.9
7th Grade
3.2
5th Grade
3.5
3rd Grade
AFFECT e.g. "When I Have a Headache, I Like to Take Aspirin."
no
yes
NO
1
YES
4
2.2
Parent
2.4
7th
2.5
5th
2.8
3rd
BRAND KNOWLEDGE e.g. "Pepto-Bismol Is: Cold Medicine, Aspirin, Cough Medicine, Stomach Medicine."
frequency of correct answers
0
12
4.0
3rd
5.7
5th
6.4
7th
6.8
Parent

Source: Compiled by the authors.

TABLE 5.2

Correlations between Illness Experience and Intent, Requests, Usage

	Third Grade	Fifth Grade	Seventh Grade	Parents
Intent	.25	.20	.26	.30
Requests	.15	.22	.27	—a
Usage	.41	.46	.50	.58

Note: All correlations significant at .01 level.
aMeans not measured.
Source: Compiled by the authors.

TABLE 5.3

Mean Scores on Medicine Behavior Indexes[a]

Variables	Third-Grade Mean (N = 221)	Fifth-Grade Mean (N = 223)	Seventh-Grade Mean (N = 229)	Parent Mean (N = 673)
Intent to take medicines when ill[b]	2.7	2.4	2.3	1.9
Medicine request frequency to parents[b]	2.8	2.5	2.2	—d
Usage of medicines[c]	2.6	2.7	2.2	1.4
Self-administration of medicines[b]	1.2	1.3	1.7	—

[a]In general, a between group difference of about 0.2 is significant at the .05 level based on Duncan multiple range test, one way ANOVAs.
[b]Means based on scale range from 1 to 4, where 4 = high.
[c]Means based on scale range from 0 to 5, where 5 = high.
[d]Means not measured.
Source: Compiled by the authors.

FIGURE 5.2

Medicine Behavior

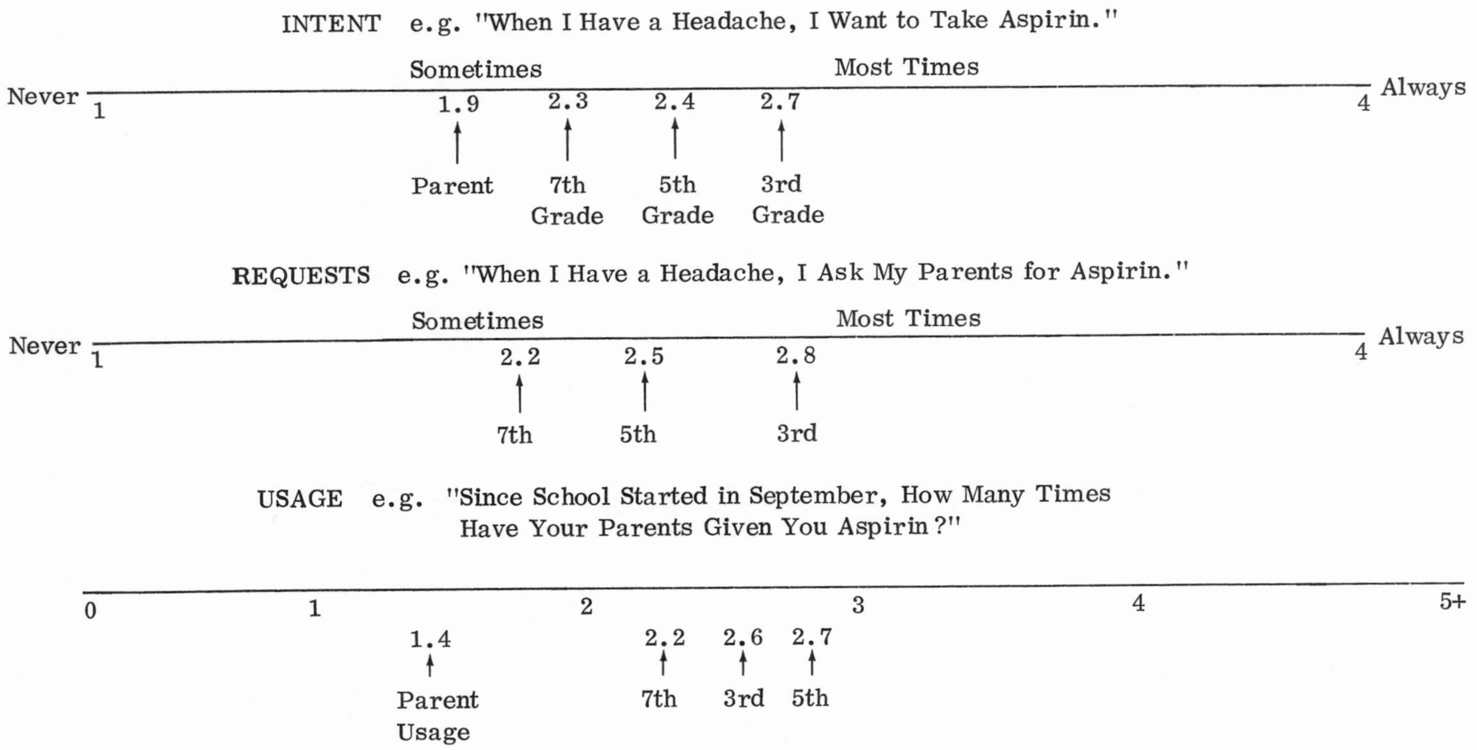

INTENT e.g. "When I Have a Headache, I Want to Take Aspirin."

Never

| | Sometimes | | | Most Times | | Always |
| 1 | | | | | | 4 |

1.9 ← Parent
2.3 ← 7th Grade
2.4 ← 5th Grade
2.7 ← 3rd Grade

REQUESTS e.g. "When I Have a Headache, I Ask My Parents for Aspirin."

Never

| | Sometimes | Most Times | Always |
| 1 | | | 4 |

2.2 ← 7th
2.5 ← 5th
2.8 ← 3rd

USAGE e.g. "Since School Started in September, How Many Times
Have Your Parents Given You Aspirin?"

| 0 | 1 | 2 | 3 | 4 | 5+ |

1.4 ← Parent Usage
2.2 ← 7th
2.6 ← 3rd
2.7 ← 5th

Source: Compiled by the authors.

53

However, given the level of relationships, the child's intent and requests to parents are obviously affected by other variables in addition to actual illness. The correlations for intent and requests may also be held down to the extent that the measures, in effect, "controlled" for illness by asking questions such as, "When I have a cold, I ask my parents for cold medicine," whereas the usage measure was a frequency count which did not contain the illness qualification phrase.

TABLE 5.4

Self-Administration of Medicines
(percent)

| | Allowed to Take without Asking | | | |
	Never	Sometimes	Most Times or Always	Total
Aspirin	67.3	16.9	15.8	100
Stomach medicine	82.5	11.7	5.8	100
Cold medicine	75.0	15.4	9.6	100
Cough medicine	70.7	18.1	11.2	100

Source: Compiled by the authors.

PARENTAL MEDIATION

What role do parents play in determining the child's medicine conceptions and usage at different social class levels? How important are parents as an information source concerning medicines and how much mediation do children report?

Parental mediation of children's medicine conceptions and behavior provides some intriguing findings. First, the actual level of parental medicine mediation will be examined. The mediation measure asked for frequency of discussions about illness and medicine since school started in September (about six months before the survey). Indications are that mediation levels (as reported by the child) are moderate. On an annual basis, the children reported an average of 3.4 discussions with parents for each topic, such as, "when you should take medicine," "medicine commercials that you see on TV," and "which medicines work the best." The number of discussions decreased somewhat by grade from 3.6 per topic at third grade to 3.4 at fifth grade and 3.1 at seventh grade.

This relatively moderate level of mediation is consistent with most socialization research findings, which indicate that mediation is generally not very deliberate nor explicit. Instead, socialization tends to be a cumulative function of many cues given out by parents over time, most of which are not verbal nor deliberate in intent (Brim and Wheeler 1966).

Now, parental mediation will be related with medicine conceptions and behavior. Results are that parental mediation shows a strong positive correlation with children's conceptions of medicine and medicine usage (Table 5.5). These results are counter to expectations. High frequency of parental medicine mediation is associated with higher reported illness levels, higher illness anxiety levels, higher perceptions of population illness incidence, more positive beliefs regarding medicine efficacy, and more positive affect toward taking medicines. There is a slight negative relationship between parental medicine mediation and brand knowledge of medicines. In terms of the medicine behavior variables, mediation level is associated positively with intent to take medicines, request frequency, usage of proprietary medicines, and the child's self-administration of medicines (among seventh graders).

The strong positive associations between mediation and medicine conceptions and behavior suggest that mediation does not act in such a way as to build critical insight but rather to accentuate acceptance and usage of medicines. This raises the obvious question as to whether mediation occurs most among parents who have strongly positive attitudes toward medicine and high usage behavior. But this is not the case. There is a lack of relationship between parental medicine mediation and parental attitudes and behavior, as the following indicates:

Parental medicine beliefs	-.03
Parental affect toward taking medicines	-.03
Parental usage of medicines	.02

It would appear, therefore, that mediation is not conducted with the intent of building either a favorable or skeptical attitude, although (see Table 5.5) it seems to have the former effect. Furthermore, mediation is not related to parental control over the child's self-administration of medicines ($r = .02$). Apparently, frequency of discussion about illness and medicine (independent of content) acts mainly to reinforce positive medicine conceptions and medicine usage.

TABLE 5.5

Partial Correlations

Variables	Parental Medicine Mediation (Controlling for Grade)	Parental Medicine Mediation (Controlling for Grade and Illness Experience)	Social Class (Controlling for Grade)
Illness behavior and conceptions			
Illness experience	.31[a]	—	-.11[a]
Anxiety about illness	.26[a]	.22[a]	-.19[a]
Perception of population illness experience	.20[a]	.03	-.05
Medicine conceptions			
Belief in efficacy of medicines	.12[a]	.11[a]	-.04
Affect toward taking medicines when ill	.16[a]	.14[a]	-.06
Brand knowledge of proprietary medicines	-.06	-.05	.17[a]
Medicine behavior			
Intent to take medicines	.25[a]	.19[a]	-.04
Medicine request frequency to parents	.32[a]	.27[a]	-.05
Usage of medicines	.34[a]	.23[a]	-.06
Self-administration of medicine[b]	.40[a]	.29[a]	-.06

[a] .01 level significance.
[b] Correlations for self-administration are for seventh grade only, as this is where most self-administration occurs.

Source: Compiled by the authors.

Another possibility to be examined is that mediation is a function of the child's illness experience level and that it is illness experience that invites mediation and leads to positive medicine attitudes and behavior. The first link of this argument holds quite well in that illness experience and parental medicine mediation are quite highly correlated (r = .31, significant at the .001 level). However, when we then control for illness experience, the results are generally the same as before—with some drop in magnitude (see Table 5.5). The only relationship that disappears is that between mediation and perception of population illness incidence. In conclusion, therefore, illness experience is at best only a partial explanation for the positive relationship between mediation and medicine conceptions and behavior.

A related parental variable to be examined is social class, measured in terms of education and occupation for household head. As shown in Table 5.5, social class acts to moderate very slightly child medicine conceptions and usage. Among children from higher social class families, there is significantly less illness anxiety and less reported illness experience. There is a slight but nonsignificant tendency toward less positive beliefs and affect toward medicine, less intent, lower request frequency, lower usage and lower self-administration of medicines (among seventh graders). There is also a positive and significant relationship between social class and brand knowledge.

This pattern of results suggests that highly educated parents may be slightly more successful in building critical thinking about medicines, or perhaps their children develop greater critical abilities in general. Conversely, these results raise some concern for children from less educationally privileged homes. These children appear to be more anxious about illness and get ill slightly more often.

A further question regarding parents is how important they are as a source of information about medicine for their children. As reported in Table 5.6, children see their parents and doctors as the most logical information sources about medicines, followed by television commercials. These data are essentially constant across grade levels (and, therefore, not reported in Table 5.6), although seventh graders acknowledge slightly less use of all information sources.

Next, one should ask whether parents and children in the same family have similar conceptions and behavior toward medicines. Interestingly, although the relationships are significant for the total sample, the magnitude of the relationships is small and the pattern by grade level is contrary to the fact that seventh-grade conceptions are more adultlike (Table 5.7). The highest parent-child correlation is for usage. This would be expected, since the child's usage is

TABLE 5.6

Children's Medicine Information Sources

Source	Mean Score*
Doctor	3.3
Parents	3.3
TV commercials	2.6
School nurse	2.5
TV programs	2.3
Books	2.3
Teachers	2.2
Friends	1.4

*Mean based on questions: "I find out about medicine from (my doctor)." YES $\underline{4}$ yes $\underline{3}$ no $\underline{2}$ NO $\underline{1}$.
Source: Compiled by the authors.

TABLE 5.7

Parent-Child Relationships

Variable	Zero-Order Correlations[a]			
	Total	Third Grade	Fifth Grade	Seventh Grade
Brand knowledge	.06[c]	.09	.10	.04
Beliefs	.11[b]	.11[c]	.23[b]	.03
Affect	.09[b]	.21[b]	.04	.02
Intent	.08[c]	.12[c]	.09	.05
Usage	.15[b]	.18[b]	.12[c]	.14[c]

[a]These correlations are based on asking the same questions of both children and parents.
[b]Significant at .01 level.
[c]Significant at .05 level.
Source: Compiled by the authors.

generally a behavior of parents, rather than children, given that
the incidence of child self-administration (usage) of medicines is
fairly low.

Thus, while the mean scores for children's conceptions become more similar to the parent's mean scores as the children get
older, there is little correlation of conceptions on a parent-child
dyad basis. This finding has previously been documented by John
Campbell (1974). It would appear, therefore, that children fairly
independently develop adultlike conceptions in a manner more consistent with cognitive development theory rather than role modeling
theory. This important issue is examined further in Chapter 7.
The baseline results suggest, however, that parental mediation does
not seem to operate in such a manner as to bring about parent-child
consensus on medicine conceptions.

TELEVISION EXPOSURE

How much are children exposed to proprietary medicine commercials?

Now attention shifts to the child's exposure to television in general and proprietary medicine commercials in particular. This
section focuses on exposure levels and the next section probes television advertising's relationships with medicine conceptions and
usage.

The average child in the sample viewed 4 hours of television
per day (Table 5.8). Third graders reported 5 hours viewing, fifth
graders 3.9 hours, and seventh graders 3.2 hours. These levels are
slightly higher than other available estimates. Richard Adler et al.,
for example, in an analysis of child viewing behavior, conclude that
"the average child over the past decade has watched 3 to 4 hours of
television per day" (1977, p. 13). The most recent Nielsen estimate
for 1977 is 3.7 hours per day among 6- to 11-year olds (Ratner et al.
1978, p. 51). The present study's somewhat higher estimate may be
due to the use of a self-reported viewing measure, which may encourage a certain degree of overestimation if the norm among children is positive toward television viewing. (This positive norm may
particularly be the case at the third-grade level.)

On average, a child in the sample was exposed to 718 commercials for proprietary medicines per year. This figure was determined by matching the child's reported monthly program viewing
with Broadcast Advertisers' Report* data that list commercials by

---

*The authors are indebted to Broadcast Advertisers' Reports,
Inc., for releasing these data to us.

program for the Philadelphia metropolitan area. These data were then extrapolated to an annual estimate.

TABLE 5.8

Exposure to Television and Proprietary
Medicine Commercials

Grade	Daily Television Exposure (hours)	Annual Number of Proprietary Medicine Commercials Seen*
Total	4.0	718
Third grade	5.0	789
Fifth grade	3.9	727
Seventh grade	3.2	641

*By far, the majority of commercials are 30 seconds long.
Source: Compiled by the authors.

TELEVISION ADVERTISING EFFECTS

What is the relationship between the child's exposure to proprietary medicine commercials and the child's medicine beliefs, attitudes, and behaviors?

This is an important focus of the research effort: to assess the impact of television advertising of proprietary medicines on children's medicine conceptions and behaviors. Correlation results are summarized in Table 5.9. In general, medicine commercial exposure shows positive and significant relationships with medicine conceptions and behaviors. More specifically, the following conclusions can be drawn (based on the first-order correlations that control for grade).

Medicine commercial exposure is positively related to illness experience ($r = .11$). It is not clear whether children who see a lot of medicine commercials think of themselves as ill more often or whether children who are ill more often watch more television. The latter seems more reasonable. Exposure is positively related to illness anxiety ($r = .22$). Again, the direction of causality is in question. Does exposure to medicine commercials build illness anxiety or does illness anxiety lead to greater television exposure? This question is examined further in Chapter 7.

TABLE 5.9

Medicine Commercial Exposure Relationships

Variables	Zero-Order Correlations	First-Order Correlations (Controlling for Grade)
Illness behavior and conceptions		
Illness experience	.13[a]	.11[a]
Anxiety about illness	.25[a]	.22[a]
Perception of population		
illness experience	.01	.00
Medicine conceptions		
Belief in efficacy of medicines	.17[a]	.12[a]
Affect toward taking medicines		
when ill	.16[a]	.13[a]
Brand knowledge of proprietary		
medicines	-.15[a]	-.09[a]
Medicine behavior		
Intent to take medicines	.18[a]	.16[a]
Medicine request frequency		
to parents	.25[a]	.22[a]
Usage of medicines	.08[b]	.06[b]
Self-administration of medicine	.23[a]	—[c]

[a].01 level significance.
[b].05 level significance.
[c]Correlations for self-administration are for seventh grade only, as this is where most self-administration occurs.
Source: Compiled by the authors.

There is a lack of relationship between exposure and the child's perception of population illness incidence. This is counter to expectation, in line with George Gerbner and Larry Gross (1976), that television can build a high estimate of population illness because of the considerable depiction of illness on television, both in doctor shows and in medicine commercials.

Medicine commercial exposure is positively related to belief in the efficacy of medicine (r = .12). This is also shown in cross-tabulation form in Table 5.10. It seems reasonable to conclude that the direction is from exposure to beliefs rather than the reverse.

TABLE 5.10

Medicine Commercial Exposure and Belief in the Efficacy of Medicines

Belief in Efficacy of Medicines[b]	Television Exposure[a] (percent)					
	High			Low		
	Third Grade	Fifth Grade	Seventh Grade	Third Grade	Fifth Grade	Seventh Grade
High	80.0	58.6	36.5	69.4	47.3	19.3
Low	20.0	41.4	63.5	30.6	52.7	80.7

[a]High-low based on median split for each grade level.
[b]High-low based on median split for total children sample.
Source: Compiled by the authors.

TABLE 5.11

Medicine Commercial Exposure and Affect toward Taking Medicines

Affect toward Taking Medicines[b]	Television Exposure[a] (percent)					
	High			Low		
	Third Grade	Fifth Grade	Seventh Grade	Third Grade	Fifth Grade	Seventh Grade
High	71.8	44.1	44.3	54.1	39.3	35.1
Low	28.2	55.9	55.7	45.9	60.7	64.9

[a]High-low based on median split for each grade level.
[b]High-low based on median split for total children sample.
Source: Compiled by the authors.

Similarly, exposure is positively related to affect (Table 5.11) toward taking medicine (r = .13). Again, the logical relationship is from exposure to affects.

Exposure is negatively related to brand knowledge—matching medicines with symptoms (r = -.09). This finding is counter to expectation. Conceivably, proprietary medicine commercials may misinform more than they inform, an inference that could be derived from Earle Barcus's (1976) content analysis of proprietary commercials, which indicates a considerable degree of multiuse emphasis.

Exposure is positively related to intent to take medicines when ill (r = .16). This relationship would logically seem to be from exposure to intent. Exposure is positively related to requests (r = .22). This is one of the strongest relationships (Table 5.12) and is really the best behavioral measure of television advertising's effects, as requesting medicine is as far as the child can go when the parent actually administers the medicines for most children.

TABLE 5.12

Medicine Commercial Exposure and Medicine Request
Frequency to Parents

| Medicine Request Frequency[b] | Television Exposure[a] (percent) | | | | | |
| | High | | | Low | | |
	Third Grade	Fifth Grade	Seventh Grade	Third Grade	Fifth Grade	Seventh Grade
High	73.6	59.5	40.0	59.5	42.9	31.6
Low	26.4	40.5	60.0	40.5	57.1	68.4

[a]High/low based on median split for each grade level.
[b]High/low based on median split for total children sample.
Source: Compiled by the authors.

Exposure is positively, although only slightly, related to usage (r = .06). This would seem to be the residue of children's requests after parents yield to or deny these requests. Exposure is positively and significantly related to children's self-administration of medicines among seventh graders (r = .23). This is convincing evidence of an exposure-behavior relationship among older children.

FURTHER ANALYSIS

In the following chapters discussion will go beyond the base-line data. Chapter 6 examines the impact of proprietary medicine advertising on special subgroups of children, such as highly anxious children and disadvantaged children. Chapter 7 examines in detail the parent-child mediation process. And Chapter 8 analyzes the relative contribution of proprietary medicine advertising as one of a number of factors explaining children's medicine beliefs, attitudes, and behavior.

REFERENCES

Adler, Richard P, et al. 1977. Research on the Effects of Television Advertising on Children. Washington, D.C.: U.S. Government Printing Office.

Barcus, G. Earle. 1976. "Over-the-Counter and Proprietary Drug Advertising on Television." In Communication Research and Drug Education, edited by Ronald E. Ostman, vol. 3, pp. 89-111. Beverly Hills, Calif.: Sage Publications.

Brim, O. G., and S. Wheeler. 1966. Socialization After Childhood: Two Essays. New York: Wiley.

Campbell, John D. 1974. "Illness Is a Point of View: The Development of Children's Concepts of Illness." Child Development 46, 92-100.

Gerbner, George, and Larry P. Gross. 1976. "Living with Television: The Violence Profile." Journal of Communication 26, 173-99.

Ratner, Ellis M., et al. 1978. FTC Staff Report on Television Advertising to Children. Washington, D.C.: Federal Trade Commission.

6

ANALYSIS OF POTENTIALLY
VULNERABLE SUBGROUPS

This chapter examines the possibility that certain subgroups of children are more strongly affected than others by exposure to television advertising for proprietary medicines. The subgroups identify children who might a priori be considered differentially susceptible to televised medicine advertising: young children, children from low education households, children who suffer most frequently from the types of illnesses for which proprietary medicines are intended, children who report higher than average anxiety about these illnesses, and older children who are sometimes allowed to self-administer proprietary medicine.

The five subgroups are not necessarily mutually exclusive. However, policy implications are made clearer by examining relatively large and easily identifiable subgroups of children based on single classificatory variables, rather than by examining the smaller and more complexly defined subgroups that result when multiple identifying variables are used.

SUBGROUP HYPOTHESES

Young Children

It is generally assumed that television advertising has stronger effects on young children than it does on older children. Attitude measures show this pattern, although behavioral measures have generally failed to reveal differential effects by age (Rossiter 1979). Nevertheless, the prevailing argument regarding advertising's greater impact on young children is that young children have not developed adequate cognitive defenses against advertising. This argument was followed by hypothesizing that younger children in the study would reveal stronger relationships than older children between medicine advertising exposure and beliefs, affect, intention and requests for medicines, but not usage of medicines, as the latter is under parental rather than child control.

Low Parental Education

Despite several studies that suggest that parental concern about television advertising's effects on children does not vary by education level, the feeling persists that children whose parents are less well educated than most are likely to receive poorer instruction about advertising techniques and about how to choose products than children of better educated parents (Adler et al. 1977). If so, televised medicine advertising may have a greater impact on children in the "disadvantaged" parental education subgroup. It was hypothesized that children from families in which the primary head of household had not completed high school would reveal stronger relationships between medicine advertising exposure and attitudes and requests than children from families in which the primary head of household is a high school graduate.

High Illness Frequency

It is reasonable to expect children who suffer frequently from common illnesses to request and use proprietary medicines more often than other children. To the extent that these products are effective, these children should also exhibit more favorable attitudes toward proprietary medicines. These tendencies would be quite independent of televised medicine advertising. However, medicine advertising may generate considerable attention among children who are frequently ill because such ads are presumably informative about illness relief. Reinforcement of this type may increase children's attitudes toward proprietary medicines (especially via the well-known placebo effect) and simultaneously may lower the threshold for children's requests for proprietary medicines when symptoms occur. In short, advertising may enhance the frequently ill child's "natural" disposition toward proprietary medicines. Accordingly, it was hypothesized that frequently ill children would reveal stronger relationships between televised medicine advertising exposure and attitudes and requests than children with a lower illness frequency.

High Illness Anxiety

Some children are much more anxious about contracting common illnesses than other children. Illness anxiety has been shown to correlate substantially with general anxiety (Brodie 1974) and general anxiety, in turn, has frequently been found to mediate persuasion. Interestingly, many persuasion studies have used the illness-oriented manifest anxiety scale (Taylor 1956) to measure general anxiety. Although the role of anxiety in persuasion is far from straightforward (McGuire 1969), both the Yale communication paradigm (Janis 1954) and the Hullian performance theory (Weiss 1968) suggest that with fairly simple messages, such as might be represented by the typical medicine commercial, persuasion effects will be stronger among high anxiety subjects. By persuasion effects is meant attitudes (cf. Janis) and also behavioral performance (cf. Hullian drive theory as described by Weiss). Borrowing from these theoretical foundations, it was hypothesized that children who exhibit high illness anxiety would reveal stronger relationships between medicine advertising exposure and attitudes and requests than children with low illness anxiety.

Self-Administration

Older children are sometimes allowed by their parents to self-administer proprietary medicines. It was found that 68 percent of the seventh-grade children (12 to 13 years old) in the sample were, at least "sometimes," permitted to take one or more proprietary medicines without asking their parents. The incidence of self-administration was low among third- and fifth-grade children. Only 26 percent of third graders were ever permitted to self-administer medicines and only 36 percent of fifth graders. For all grades, this self-administration is usually for aspirin and in the response category of "sometimes" rather than "most times" or "always." As parental control over medicine usage lessens, it might be expected that televised medicine advertising's effects on children's attitudes would be reflected in their usage behavior.

Charles Atkin (1975) found a nonsignificant correlation between medicine advertising exposure and usage for his fifth- through seventh-grade sample (see Chapter 3). However, Milavsky et al. (1975-76), studying teenagers, found a small but significant correlation. It was therefore hypothesized that a stronger relationship between medicine advertising exposure and proprietary medicine usage would be observed for older children who are allowed to self-administer proprietary medicines than for children who are not

permitted to self-administer these products. It is worth noting
that this is the only subgroup in which a usage effect is predicted.
All other predictions are confined to attitudes and requests.

METHODOLOGY AND STATISTICAL PROCEDURE

Five subgroups were identified on the basis of age, parental
education, illness frequency, illness anxiety, and self-administration,
respectively.

The young children's subgroup comprised third-grade children (ages
8 to 9), whose responses were compared with those of fifth and
seventh graders (ages 10 to 13).

The low parental education subgroup comprised the 20 percent of
children from families in which the primary head of household
had not completed high school.

The high illness subgroup comprised the highest scoring quartile on
the illness experience index. These children reported an illness
symptom at least every two weeks (average frequency of greater
than 3.7 on the 0 to 5 index).

The high anxiety subgroup comprised the highest scoring quartile on
the illness anxiety index. It should be noted that the overall level
of illness anxiety observed in the sample was low: the cutoff for
the high anxiety quartile was only 2.0 on the 1 to 4 index (mid-
point = 2.5); thus, the high anxiety subgroup more accurately consists of relatively or moderately anxious children rather than
extremely anxious children.

The self-administration subgroup comprised the 68 percent of
seventh-grade children (ages 12 to 13) who checked other than
the "never" category on the medicine control index; that is, those
who reported being allowed to take one or more proprietary medicines at least "sometimes" without asking their parents.

The statistical procedure for the subgroups' analysis is similar to that for the baseline results reported in Chapter 5, with several exceptions. The exceptions are as follows:

The present analysis is based on 668 children rather than the full
673. This was necessitated by the inclusion of head of household
education level as a subgroup variable, a measure for which five
cases had missing data. The present analysis is therefore based
on complete data for all variables used to identify the subgroups.

A second difference is that the correlations reported in this chapter
are all corrected statistically for the effects of measurement

reliability (Guilford 1954; Nunnally 1978). Table 6.1 indicates the effect of this correction: basically it has the effect of increasing the "raw" correlations slightly, thus providing better estimates of the relationships between medicine advertising exposure and the outcome variables by allowing for less than perfectly reliable measures (see Table 4.2).

TABLE 6.1

Correlations[a] of Proprietary Medicine Advertising Exposure with Medicine Attitudes and Behavior for the Total Sample[b]

Dependent Variables	Total Sample (N = 668)	
	Uncorrected	Corrected[c]
Belief	12[d]	16[d]
Affect	13[d]	17[d]
Intent	16[d]	21[d]
Requests	22[d]	30[d]
Usage	06[f]	10[e]

[a]Controlling for grade (see text).
[b]Decimal points omitted for clarity.
[c]Corrected for attenuation by the formula

$$Cr_{xy} = r_{xy} / \sqrt{r_{xx}} \sqrt{r_{xy}} .$$

[d]$p < .001$.
[e]$p \leq .005$.
[f]$p \leq .05$.
Source: Compiled by the authors.

Third, when the subgroup results span grade levels, the correlations are additionally corrected for age trends (first-order partials). This provides a "downward" correction for the correlations, necessitated by the realization, from the baseline results in Chapter 5, that because medicine advertising exposure and medicine attitudes decline jointly as a function of the child's age, a partially spurious direct correlation between the two would otherwise result.

Reference is made in the analysis to "practically significant" correlations, which are larger than the statistically significant ones. The level established for inferring practical significance is $\underline{r} = .30$. This follows the practice suggested by the Surgeon General's Scientific Advisory Committee on Television and Social Behavior (1972) for identifying relationships of practical relevance to policy makers.

SUBGROUP RESULTS

In order to facilitate comparison of subgroup results with total sample results, the means and standard deviations for the total sample are shown in Table 6.2. The correlations between medicine advertising exposure and children's medicine responses by subgroup are shown in Table 6.3. The means to accompany the correlations are shown in Table 6.4. Subgroup correlations were compared via 1-tailed t-tests, using Fisher's r to z transformation, as directional hypotheses were at issue. Subgroup means were compared with 2-tailed t-tests for descriptive purposes only, because no directional hypotheses were explicitly advanced in relation to mean differences.

TABLE 6.2

Mean Levels of Proprietary Medicine Attitudes and Behavior and Medicine Advertising Exposure for the Total Sample[a]

Dependent Variables	Total Sample (N = 668)	
	Mean	Standard Deviation
Belief	3.2	.6
Affect	2.6	.8
Intent	2.5	.8
Requests	2.5	.8
Usage	2.5	1.3
Medicine advertising exposure[b]	13.8	8.2

[a]Range for first four measures is 1 to 4, with 4 = highest. Range for usage is 0 to 5, with 5 = highest.
[b]Measured in terms of number of 30-second drug commercials per week.
Source: Compiled by the authors.

TABLE 6.3

Correlations of Proprietary Medicine Advertising Exposure with
Medicine Attitudes and Behavior for the Subgroups[a]

	Age		Parental Education		Illness Frequency		Illness Anxiety		Self-Administration[b]	
	Younger (N = 218)	Older (N = 450)	Low (N = 132)	High (N = 529)	High (N = 171)	Low (N = 497)	High (N = 166)	Low (N = 502)	None (N = 74)	Some (N = 155)
Belief	-02	28[c]	06	20[c]	23[c]	13[d]	26[c]	07[f]	29[e]	.23[d]
Affect	22[c]	14[c]	13[f]	17[c]	28[c]	12[d]	39[c]	02	26[f]	.12
Intent	29[c]	16[c]	44[c]	12[d]	15[f]	22[c]	43[c]	09[f]	23[f]	.19[e]
Requests	26[c]	33[c]	39[c]	27[c]	25[c]	30[c]	43[c]	21[c]	34[d]	.33[c]
Usage	03	15[c]	12[f]	10[d]	-00	09[f]	04	07[f]	'23[f]	.38[c]

[a]Decimal points omitted for clarity. All correlations have been corrected for attenuation by the formula: corrected $r_{xy} = r_{xy} / (\sqrt{r_{xx}} \sqrt{r_{yy}})$. Also, all correlations except those for the younger subgroup, that is, third graders, have been partialled for grade level (see text). Underlined correlations indicate significant subgroup differences.

[b]Seventh grade only.

[c]p < .001.

[d]p < .005.

[e]p < .01.

[f]p < .05.

Source: Compiled by the authors.

TABLE 6.4

Mean Levels of Proprietary Medicine Attitudes and Behavior and
Medicine Advertising Exposure for the Subgroups[a]

	Age		Parental Education		Illness Frequency		Illness Anxiety		Self-Administration[b]	
	Younger (N = 218)	Older (N = 450)	Low (N = 132)	High (N = 529)	High (N = 171)	Low (N = 497)	High (N = 166)	Low (N = 502)	None (N = 74)	Some (N = 155)
Belief	3.5	3.0	3.2	3.2	3.3	3.2	3.5	3.1	2.9	2.9
Affect	2.8	2.4	2.6	2.6	2.7	2.5	2.9	2.5	2.3	2.4
Intent	2.7	2.4	2.6	2.4	2.7	2.4	2.6	2.4	2.1	2.4
Requests	2.8	2.4	2.5	2.5	2.7	2.4	2.7	2.4	2.3	2.2
Usage	2.6	2.4	2.5	2.5	3.2	2.4	2.7	2.4	2.1	2.3
Medicine advertising exposure[c]	15.2	13.1	17.2	12.9	15.2	13.3	17.2	12.7	13.7	11.7

[a]Range for first four measures is 1 to 4, with 4 = highest. Range for usage is 0 to 5, with 5 = highest. Underlined means indicate significant subgroup differences.
[b]Seventh grade only.
[c]Measured in terms of number of 30-second drug commercials per week.
Source: Compiled by the authors.

Although primary focus is on the correlations between exposure and outcomes for each of the five subgroups, these correlations are placed in context by first describing the mean results.

Young Children

Young children are exposed to televised medicine advertising at a higher rate than older children, presumably because they watch more television. As shown in Table 6.4, the difference amounts to about two more medicine commercials a week (15.2 versus 13.1, $p < .05$). Also, although their rate of usage of proprietary medicines is not significantly higher than that of older children ($p > .10$), young children exhibit significantly more favorable attitudes toward, and requests for, these products (all $p < .001$). Young children are therefore exposed to more televised medicine advertising (on a current basis) than are older children and have stronger dispositions toward proprietary medicines.

However, the correlational results do not indicate that young children are more strongly influenced than older children by televised medicine advertising. As shown in Table 6.3, young children exhibited a stronger advertising-related correlation on only one measure: intent to take proprietary medicines when symptoms occur ($r = .29$ versus $r = .16$ for older children, $p < .05$). On three of the five measures, the age differences were in the opposite direction. These included the requests measure, for which a practically significant correlation was found for the older children ($r = .33$, $p < .001$). The belief and usage correlations also suggest stronger televised medicine advertising influence among older children, although it should be stressed that the differences by age group are not statistically significant. In general, the results do not support the hypothesis that younger children are more strongly affected by televised medicine advertising than older children.

Before turning to the other subgroup analyses, it should be noted that the significantly lower proprietary medicine dispositions observed among older children could be taken as evidence that cumulative exposure to televised medicine advertising has a slight dampening effect on children's proclivities toward proprietary medicines. The average 10- to 13-year-old child will have seen some 1,400 more medicine commercials than the average 8- to 9-year-old child, yet the older child's dispositions are lower. Of course, this trend undoubtedly reflects developmental and experiential changes in addition to cumulative exposure, but it does count against the increased susceptibility viewpoint.

Low Parental Education

Children from families in which the primary head of household did not complete high school had considerably higher exposure to televised medicine advertising than children from the remainder of the sample (17.2 medicine commercials per week versus 12.9, $p < .001$). If sheer exposure has an effect, then it would be expected that these disadvantaged children would have much more favorable dispositions toward proprietary medicines. The mean responses in Table 6.4 show that this is not the case. There are no significant differences in attitudes, requests, or proprietary medicine usage levels between low and high parental education children.

The correlational results also suggest rejection of the hypotheses that educationally disadvantaged children are more strongly influenced by televised medicine advertising. As shown in Table 6.3, there is only one significant difference (of four hypothesized) that supports this contention. However, two fairly large and practically significant correlations are observed in this subgroup: $r = .44$ for intent and $r = .39$ for requests.

A possible interpretation is that the high current exposure to televised medicine advertising among educationally disadvantaged children has a noticeable effect on these, the more immediately motivational measures. For these two measures only, exposure to medicine advertising appears to influence the degree (15 to 18 percent shared variance) but not the level of children's responses toward proprietary medicines. In other words, medicine advertising on television appears to be slightly more capable of "moving" educationally disadvantaged children's dispositions upward or downward in relation to the amount of exposure, although the net effect for the average child in this subgroup is no greater than that for other children. Thus, there is a case of high exposure, fairly high correlations (for the motivationally oriented measures), but low outcomes. This result clearly suggests rejection of the hypothesis that children from educationally disadvantaged families are excessively disposed toward proprietary medicines, although it leaves partial support for the hypothesis that such children are more strongly influenced by televised medicine advertising.

High Illness Frequency

Children who have a relatively high frequency of colds, coughs, headaches, and stomachaches, as might be expected, show a higher usage rate of proprietary medicines than other children. The usage means in Table 6.4 indicate, in everyday figures, that the more frequently ill child receives proprietary drugs about once every two weeks versus once every two and one-half weeks for other children. There is also a slight but significant tendency for frequently ill children to be exposed to more medicine advertising (15.2 drug ads a week versus 13.3, $p < .05$). Furthermore, on a "per symptom" basis, with the exception of belief in the efficacy of proprietary medicines, frequently ill children reveal significantly more favorable attitudes toward these products and are more likely to request them when symptoms occur (all $p < .01$).

Nevertheless, the correlations in Table 6.3 suggest that these dispositions are not attributable to televised medicine advertising. The only result in support of the hypothesis that frequently ill children are more strongly influenced occurred on the affect measure: medicine advertising exposure was associated with a stronger tendency to like (or not mind) taking these products when symptoms occur. Higher exposure did not, however, have a stronger effect on frequently ill children's beliefs, intentions, requests, or usage. It therefore appears that the frequently ill child sees more medicine commercials, perhaps because of greater opportunity during periods of illness, but that this child's more favorable dispositions toward proprietary medicines are largely coincidental, based possibly on favorable usage experience. This is the third instance now in which the sheer exposure contention for potentially "high risk" subgroups is discounted by the failure to find a supportive correlation pattern.

High Illness Anxiety

Illness anxiety emerges as an important mediating variable in the present study. The mean responses in Table 6.4 indicate that children with (relatively) high illness anxiety are exposed to significantly more televised medicine advertising than lower anxiety children (17.2 commercials a week versus 12.7, $p < .001$) and that they have significantly more favorable attitudes, more frequent requests, and higher usage of proprietary medicines (all $p < .001$).

The mediating role of illness anxiety is confirmed by the correlational results. As shown in Table 6.3, the high anxiety subgroup exhibited significantly larger correlations between medicine advertising exposure and belief in the efficacy of proprietary medicines ($p < .05$), affect toward taking these products ($p < .001$), intention to take them when symptoms occur ($p < .001$), and requests to parents for proprietary medicines ($p < .005$) than lower anxiety children. The latter three correlations are also of the magnitude established as being of practical significance ($r = .39$, $.43$, and $.43$, respectively), indicating that, for the one in four children with relatively high anxiety about illness, medicine advertising exposure accounts for 15 to 18 percent of the variance in their attitudes toward, and requests for, proprietary medicines.

Thus, there is the only instance in this study where higher exposure corresponds with higher dispositions and with higher correlations. High illness anxiety (relatively speaking, given the moderate cutoff established for this subgroup) appears to facilitate attitude formation, as suggested by the Yale research on generalized anxiety as a personality trait, and also to amplify behavioral responses, especially requests, as suggested by the motivational view of anxiety in Hullian performance theory. It should be emphasized, however, that anxious children do not show extreme increases in dispositions and that these children's usage of proprietary medicines, as with other children's, remains unaffected by medicine advertising exposure (based on the correlation analysis).

The causal role that illness anxiety appears to play in mediating the effect of medicine advertising on children is buttressed further by the post hoc analysis of high illness anxiety by age group shown in Table 6.5. First, high illness anxiety children tend to be younger. When the top quartile cutting point was applied within age groups it was found that 38 percent of the 8- to 9-year-olds but only 18 percent of the 10- to 13-year-olds fell into the high illness anxiety category. Although the data are cross-sectional rather than longitudinal, the apparent reduction in high illness anxiety with age suggests that exposure to medicine advertising does not "cause" illness anxiety. Remember that the average 10- to 13-year-old has had some two years' more exposure to televised medicine advertising than the average 8- to 9-year-old. The results in Table 6.5 indicate that illness anxiety lessens as the child grows older but, if the child remains anxious, as almost one in five (18 percent) does, then he or she is very likely to be influenced by medicine advertising on television. The correlations among older, high illness anxiety children, with the exception of usage, are all greater than .40, reaching .53 for intent and .54 for requests for proprietary medicines. The mean response levels for these children are also for the most part significantly higher than those of their peers (although they still do not reach extreme levels). It appears, therefore, that illness anxiety is a predisposing factor that increases the effect of televised medicine advertising on children.

Self-Administration

Children who are allowed to self-administer proprietary medicines are actually exposed to significantly less televised medicine

TABLE 6.5

Post Hoc Analysis of Illness Anxiety Correlations by Age Group[a]

| | Younger (N = 218) | | | | Older (N = 450) | | | |
| | High Illness Anxiety (N = 83) | | Low Illness Anxiety (N = 135) | | High Illness Anxiety (N = 83) | | Low Illness Anxiety (N = 367) | |
	Correlation	Mean	Correlation	Mean	Correlation	Mean	Correlation	Mean
Belief	04	3.7	-12	3.4	44[b]	3.2	18[b]	3.0
Affect	41[b]	3.2	04	2.6	42[b]	2.6	01	2.4
Intent	37[b]	2.8	22[c]	2.6	53[b]	2.5	03	2.3
Requests	36[b]	2.9	17[e]	2.7	54[b]	2.6	23[b]	2.3
Usage	21[e]	2.7	-10	2.6	-12	2.8	16[b]	2.4

[a]The first column for each subgroup shows correlations with televised medicine advertising exposure (as in Table 6.2) and the second shows mean response levels (as in Table 6.4). Significant differences within age groups are underlined.

[b]p < .001.
[c]p < .005.
[d]p < .01.
[e]p < .05.

Source: Compiled by the authors.

77

advertising than their seventh-grade peers who are not allowed to self-administer these products (11. 7 drug ads a week versus 13. 7, $p < .05$). However, the two groups exhibit similar levels of attitudes, requests, and usage. Specifically, the self-administration subgroup shows significantly stronger intentions to take proprietary medicine when symptoms occur but no greater usage (Table 6.4). The correlational results (Table 6.3) also suggest similarity between the two seventh-grade groups in terms of the extent to which medicine advertising is related to dispositions toward proprietary medicines. However, the hypothesis in this case pertains only to usage.

The self-administration subgroup shows a relatively large exposure-usage correlation ($r = .38$, $p < .001$). Although this correlation is not significantly larger than the correlation observed for seventh graders who are not allowed to self-administer proprietary medicines ($r = .23$, $p < .05$), it is significantly larger than the correlation shown earlier in the table for older children (fifth and seventh graders combined: a correlation partialled for grade level of $r = .15$, $p < .001$). The correlation of $r = .38$ for the self-administration subgroup also exceeds the level set for practical significance of $r = .30$, and indicates that just over 14 percent of these children's usage is accounted for by exposure to televised medicine advertising.

Thus, it appears as though medicine advertising has a greater effect on children's proprietary medicine usage when the usage decision is left at least some of the time to them rather than to their parents. Interestingly, this effect is achieved with lower average exposure to medicine advertising than their peers receive, which once again casts doubt on the sheer exposure argument. It is important to note, however, that these children's usage rate is not significantly higher than under parental administration conditions: about once every three weeks in both cases. This is lower, for example, than the usage rate for frequently ill children (once every two weeks) or children with high illness anxiety (once every two and one-half weeks). Consequently, older children who are allowed to self-administer proprietary medicines cannot be regarded as being more strongly influenced than other children by televised medicine advertising.

SUMMARY

The present analysis of subgroups supplements the baseline results of Chapter 5. It is as informative for what it did not find among these subgroups as well as for what it did find. The findings by subgroup may be summarized as follows.

Young children are not more strongly influenced by medicine advertising than older children. Although their higher exposure level and more favorable attitudes toward proprietary medicines would appear to suggest a stronger connection for younger children, the correlational results revealed this not to be true. Young children simply seem to be more favorably disposed toward TV viewing and, separately, toward proprietary medicines than older children.

Children from low parental education ("disadvantaged") households are somewhat more strongly influenced by medicine advertising than more privileged children, but do not show more favorable attitudes toward these medicines. Medicine advertising exposure is high in the disadvantaged subgroup, and it does relate quite strongly to disadvantaged children's attitudes toward medicines. However, their net attitudes toward proprietary medicines are no more favorable than those of nondisadvantaged children.

Frequently ill children, defined as the 25 percent reporting common illness symptoms more often than their peers, are not more strongly influenced by medicine advertising than children who are less often ill. The frequently ill child is exposed to more advertising, perhaps because of periods of illness, and also has more favorable attitudes toward proprietary medicines, perhaps because of favorable experience with these products; but the correlational results again suggest that these are relatively separate phenomena. The correlations between exposure and attitudes are no higher for frequently ill children than they are for children who are less often ill. Without higher correlations, it cannot be concluded that medicine advertising has a greater impact on the frequently ill child.

Children who exhibit relatively high anxiety about contracting common illnesses, defined as the 25 percent with the highest scores on the illness anxiety index, are more strongly influenced by medicine advertising than other children. Anxious children are exposed to more medicine commercials, have more favorable attitudes toward proprietary medicines, and exhibit stronger exposure–attitude correlations than their less anxious peers. The coincidence of absolute and correlational results suggests that illness anxiety is a significant factor mediating between medicine advertising exposure and medicine attitudes. However, despite the anxious child's relatively greater apparent susceptibility to medicine advertising, no evidence of extreme effects was found for this subgroup, nor for any of the others defined on the basis of age, parental education, and illness frequency.

Finally, older children who are allowed to self-administer proprietary medicines on occasion do not show increased usage of these products. Their usage rate is more strongly affected by medicine advertising than children whose usage is fully controlled by parents, but their usage remains at the same level. Thus, with full parental control, and even without it, when there is greater freedom for the child to make the choice, proprietary medicine usage stays moderate.

REFERENCES

Adler, R. P., et al. 1977. "The Effects of Television Advertising on Children." Washington, D.C.: National Science Foundation.

Atkin, C. K. 1975. "The Effects of Television Advertising on Children: Survey of Pre-Adolescent's Responses to Television Commercials." A report submitted to Office of Child Development, Department of Health, Education, and Welfare.

Brodie, B. 1974. "Views of Healthy Children Toward Illness." American Journal of Public Health 64, 1156-59.

Guilford, J. P. 1954. Psychometric Methods. 2nd ed. New York: McGraw-Hill.

Janis, I. L. 1954. "Personality Correlates of Susceptibility to Persuasion." Journal of Personality 22, 504-18.

McGuire, W. J. 1969. "Attitudes and Attitude Change." In The Handbook of Social Psychology, edited by G. Lindzey and E. Aronson, 2nd ed., vol. 3, pp. 136-314. Reading, Mass.: Addison-Wesley.

Milavsky, J. R., B. Pekowsky, and H. Stipp. 1975-76. "TV Drug Advertising and Proprietary and Illicit Drug Use Among Teenage Boys." Public Opinion Quarterly 39 (Winter): 457-81.

Nunnally, J. C. 1978. Psychometric Theory. 2nd ed. New York: McGraw-Hill.

Rossiter, J. R. 1977. "TV Advertising's General Impact on Children." Journal of Advertising Research, in press.

Surgeon General's Scientific Advisory Committee on Television and Social Behavior. 1972. Television and Growing Up: The Impact of Televised Violence. Washington, D.C.: U.S. Government Printing Office.

Taylor, J. A. 1956. "Drive Theory and Manifest Anxiety."
Psychological Bulletin 53, 303-20.

Weiss, Robert F. 1968. "An Extension of Hullian Learning Theory
to Persuasive Communication." In Psychological Foundations of
Attitudes, edited by Anthony G. Greenwald, et al., pp. 109-46.
New York: Academic Press.

7

PARENTAL INFLUENCE

The purpose of this chapter is to examine in more detail the relationship between parents' and children's conceptions of proprietary medicines. The commonsense expectation is that children's proprietary medicine attitudes and usage propensities are strongly influenced by parental attitudes and usage. However, the preliminary analysis of parent-child baseline results (as discussed in Chapter 5) suggested that parental influence on children's attitudes and usage may be small. Should this tendency be maintained under the more detailed analysis presented in the present chapter, which examines parent and child attitudes and usage for each category of proprietary medicines individually rather than in terms of the summary indexes used previously, one would have to conclude that children develop their conceptions of proprietary medicines largely independently of parental influences, that is, on the basis of their own experience.

There is plenty of evidence from prior studies to support the expectation of a substantial parent-child influence process (this shall be referred to as the correspondence model). However, there is also some new evidence that contradicts this expectation (referred to as the independence model). In fact, recent commentators from the fields of sociology (Skolnick 1978) and cognitive development (Gelman 1978) have suggested that the traditionally assumed influence of parents may be overestimated and the independent abilities of children underestimated. The evidence in favor of both the correspondence and independence positions will be briefly reviewed.

THE CORRESPONDENCE MODEL

The most prevalent viewpoint in the health and medical literature is that children's conceptions of common illnesses and the

82

treatment thereof via self-medication correspond closely with the views of their parents. This viewpoint, which may be described as the correspondence model, is amply reflected in an extensive review of the family's role in health and medical care by Theodor Litman (1974), who notes:

> In addition to performing such basic functions as biological reproduction, emotional development, socialization, the organization of statuses and roles and relationships within the community, the family constitutes perhaps the most important social context within which illness occurs and is resolved. (p. 495)

Litman cites many studies that appear to support the direct role of the family in influencing children's health and medical attitudes and behavior, and the following brief review draws mainly from his compendium of studies.

The importance of family influence is indicated, for example, by the finding that for common illnesses typically treated by proprietary medicines administered in the home, such as colds, coughs, headaches, and stomachaches, family members are far more likely to be consulted than are physicians or pharmacists (Knapp, Knapp, and Engle 1966; Richardson 1970). Litman's own research found that the family member most often consulted was the mother (65 percent of instances) rather than the father (16 percent) or both mother and father (13 percent). Litman (1971) also found that adults report obtaining their own health attitudes and opinions most frequently from their parents (42 percent) rather than their spouses (15 percent), health personnel (15 percent), or mass media sources (8 percent).

Opportunities for family discussion of illnesses and their treatment would seem to be reasonably prevalent. In a survey of low-income families, Joel Alpert and co-workers (1967) found that the average individual family member reported an illness symptom every 13 days and the average family as a group reported a symptom every 3 days, with children heavily represented in these figures. No comparable studies could be found for middle- and upper-income families, but in these families, too, it seems likely that common illnesses and their treatment are a fairly frequent topic of discussion, particularly, it may be inferred, mother-child discussion.

The studies cited above suggest that the process of parent-to-child transmission of illness and proprietary medicine usage information is well established. What is not well established is the outcome of the transmission process. For example, many adults hold negative attitudes toward the use of drugs and medicines, proprietary or otherwise, for the treatment of colds, coughs, headaches, stomachaches, and other common illnesses. Statistics from a recent commercial survey of some 2,000 adults (Target Group Index, 1975) are interesting in this respect and are reproduced in Table 7.1. It can be inferred that for each symptom about 25 percent of adults appear not to take medication to treat common illnesses. On the other hand, although these results do not show whether people always take a remedy when symptoms occur, or whether they do so only in certain instances, about 75 percent of adults appear to be in favor of using medication to treat common illnesses.

TABLE 7.1

General Incidence of Common Illnesses and
Medicine Usage among Adults

Illness	Suffer From (percent)	Take Remedy (percent)
Headaches	40	31
Colds	25	19
Indigestion, upset stomach	23	17
Coughs, sore throats	18	14

Source: Target Group Index, Miscellaneous Drug Products. Report P-20 (New York: Axiom Market Research Bureau, 1975).

Even if adult attitudes and usage patterns are known, however, there is no guarantee that they, as parents, will transmit these attitudes and usage patterns to their children. While it seems likely that parents in favor of proprietary medicines would communicate these favorable feelings, either directly or indirectly, to children and that parents opposed to proprietary medicines would communicate unfavorable feelings, numerous exceptions can be conceived. These potential exceptions to the commonsense correspondence model are described in the formulation of a second, competing model.

THE INDEPENDENCE MODEL

Parents and children may exhibit independent attitudes toward proprietary medicine usage for a number of reasons. Parents may say nothing to their children about proprietary medicines. Although this seems unlikely from Litman's review, silence on the part of parents would leave children to form their own conclusions based on experience and other information, such as mass media advertising. Another possibility is that parents may not communicate their own true attitudes to children, a sort of "do as I say, not as I do" phenomenon. Yet a third possibility is that parents do communicate their true attitudes to children but that this communication does not have much influence. Children may listen to parents but simultaneously form their own attitudes, which dominate and produce an independent result when parent and child attitudes and behavior are compared. Although these are three quite different processes, they all could lead to the same outcome, an outcome that may be described as the independence model.

Evidence for the independence model comes from a study by John Campbell (1975). The study focused on the similarity between mothers' and children's conceptions of illness. The main question asked of respondents, 264 6- to 12-year-old children and their mothers, was "How do you know when you are sick?" The study is relevant to the present one because children and parents must presumably agree on illness definition before action can be taken, that is, administering a proprietary medicine.

Content analysis of the responses produced 11 reliably coded themes underlying illness conceptions. When the aggregate group profiles of mothers' and children's responses across the 11 themes were compared, Campbell found a high correlation ($r = .59$, $p < .05$). This aggregate correspondence appeared to increase as the children became older ($r = .43$ for children aged 6 up to $9\frac{1}{2}$; $r = .69$ for those aged $9\frac{1}{2}$ to 12). However, when responses were compared on a direct dyadic basis, that is, with mother-child pairs as the unit of analysis, the correlations for 10 of the 11 themes turned out to be nonsignificant (the other was $r = .13$) and there were no differences by age. Across all 11 themes making up mothers' and children's conception of illness, the total correlation computed on an intra-family basis was essentially zero ($r = .01$, n.s.). Campbell (1975) concluded that:

> the data of the present study do not support the view that children's definitions of illness directly result from maternal tuition. . . . The developing definitional consensus evident in comparisons of group profiles may be

less a reflection of direct interpersonal learning than
it is a process of general social accretion that keeps
pace with cognitive development. (p. 99)

Campbell's study supplies provocative evidence for the independence model, but there are several limitations that should be
noted. For one, the children were all short-term patients in a
pediatric hospital. Thus it is possible that these children may have
had a somewhat greater opportunity than nonhospitalized children to
develop their own views about illness, aided also, perhaps, by
comments made by medical staff. Additionally, and more impor-
tantly from the perspective of the present research, Campbell's
study dealt only with the "need base" for proprietary medicines,
that is, illness definition, and not with parents' or children's attitudes toward the medicines themselves or their actual usage of
them. The independence model in these regards, as with the correspondence model, remains untested.

THE PRESENT ANALYSIS

The present analysis compares parents and their children in
terms of a number of major variables relating to proprietary medicine attitudes and usage. The variables can be conceptualized in
terms of a need-disposition-behavior framework suggested by
Litman (1974): illness frequency (need), attitude toward use of
proprietary medicines (disposition), and actual usage (behavior).
In this study the researchers are interested in (1) Whether
child and parental diagnoses of the child's frequency of illness correspond and whether these diagnoses, in turn, are influenced by
parental illness. (2) Whether children's attitudes toward the use of
proprietary medicines for treating the illness correspond with
parental attitudes. Attitudes in this study are operationalized in
terms of belief in the efficacy of proprietary medicines, affect toward taking medicines, and intention to take medicines when illness
symptoms occur. Examined also is the child's tendency to request
proprietary medicines from parents when illness symptoms occur.
(3) Whether children's actual usage of proprietary medicines corresponds with parental assessment of children's usage and whether
children's usage, in turn, is influenced by parental usage. These
"dependent" variables are summarized in Table 7.2.
The variables just described measure the outcomes but not the
process of parent-child influence pertaining to need, disposition,
and usage. To illuminate the process by which outcomes may occur
three "independent" variables were examined: age of child, parent-

child mediation (that is, parent-child discussions about illness and proprietary medicines), and the child's exposure to television advertising for proprietary medicines.

TABLE 7.2

Child and Parent "Dependent" Variables
Employed in the Present Study

	Child Variables	Parental Assessment of Child Variables	Parent Variables
Need			
Illness frequency (by major symptom types)	x	x	x
Disposition			
Belief in the efficacy of proprietary medicines	x	N.R.[a]	x
Affect toward taking proprietary medicines	x	N.R.	x
Intent to take proprietary medicines	x	N.R.	x
Request tendency for proprietary medicines	x	x	N.A.[b]
Behavior			
Usage frequency of proprietary medicines	x	x	x

Note: x = measured variables.
[a]Not relevant because children's dispositions, in contrast with overt behavior, are not observable by parents.
[b]Not applicable because requests are a child-response only.
Source: Compiled by the authors.

Age of child was included because if there is a process underlying parental influence then this should become evident over time. For example, if the correspondence model were true, parents would have more opportunities to influence children as they grow older, so correspondence should increase. Conversely, if the independence model were true, older children would have a longer period to develop their own attitude and usage patterns based on personal experience, so independence should increase. Analysis by age group provides insight on these potential processes.

Parent-child mediation, representing frequency of parent-child discussions about illness and proprietary medicines, was included as a means of further illuminating the influence process. Should the correspondence model hold true, a high contribution from the parent-child mediation variable would indicate that parental influence is a relatively overt process based on frequency of discussion about illness and medicines; whereas a low contribution would suggest that parents influence children by example rather than by direct instruction.

Conversely, should the independence model hold true, the role of parent-child mediation will allow one to infer which of the three processes described in conjunction with this model may have produced the independent outcome. A high contribution of parent-child mediation to children's attitudes and usage, in conjunction with independent parental attitudes and usage, would suggest the "do as I say, not as I do" phenomenon in which parents do not communicate their true attitudes to their children. A low contribution of parent-child mediation to children's attitudes and usage, again in conjunction with independence, would suggest the "say nothing" explanation, whereby children are left largely to their own initiative in learning about proprietary medicines.

Between these two extremes, a moderate contribution of parent-child mediation to children's attitudes and usage, once more in the presence of independent parental attitudes and usage, would suggest that children listen to parents but simultaneously form their own opinions, which predominate when parent and child attitudes and behavior are compared.

Exposure to television advertising for proprietary medicines was included as a potential source of children's proclivities toward these products. Exposure may work to influence: need definition, by drawing the child's attention to apparent illness symptoms; dispositions, by portraying proprietary medicines as effective and appropriate remedies for these illnesses; and behavior, by reminding children to use these products. The small but significant role of televised medicine advertising previously identified in Chapters 5 and 6 indicated that it should be reexamined in the parent-child context as a source that potentially competes with parents as an influence on children's proprietary attitudes and behavior.

Sample

The present analysis seeks to examine parent and child variables at the level of specific illness symptoms and specific medicine types, that is, for colds, coughs, headaches, and stomachaches separately. Hence, the original variables, rather than the composite indexes used in Chapters 5 and 6, are employed. This means that no missing data can be included; consequently, the present analysis is based on 612 complete mother-child dyads (1,224 respondents in total) rather than on the 673 children for whom the index measures were available in the previous analyses. As expected, younger children have a slightly higher incidence of missing data. However, the resulting sample of dyads still provides a fairly equal distribution by grade level: third grade (N = 190), fifth grade (N = 209), and seventh grade (N = 213).

Aggregate Results

Campbell (1975) found a fairly high degree of correspondence between the responses of children in aggregate and parents in aggregate, especially as children grow older. This was confirmed in the present study in that there is a significant developmental trend in children's illness frequency, dispositions toward proprietary medicines, and usage levels such that they become more adultlike as they grow older (recognizing that this is a longitudinal inference from cross-sectional data). These aggregate results, averaged across symptoms for economy of presentation, are shown in Figure 7.1.

It can be seen that illness frequency disposition and behavior (usage) all decline with age: respective linear F values (d.f. 3 1219) for the five one-way ANOVAs are all significant at $p < .0001$; there are also some smaller but significant deviations from linearity in the case of illness frequency, beliefs, and usage that are evident in the figure. As children grow older, then, they tend as a group to exhibit adult patterns in that illness frequency declines, as do their attitudes toward the use of proprietary medicines and their actual usage.

Dyadic Results

In order to examine parent-child influence on an intrafamily basis, the unit of analysis becomes the dyad. Each of the 612

FIGURE 7.1

Aggregate Response Trends for Children (by Age Group) and Parents for Illness,
Proprietary Medicine Attitudes, and Usage

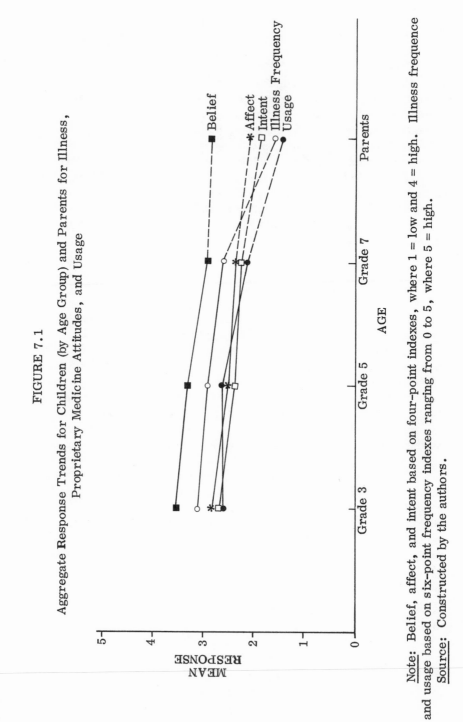

Note: Belief, affect, and intent based on four-point indexes, where 1 = low and 4 = high. Illness frequence and usage based on six-point frequency indexes ranging from 0 to 5, where 5 = high.

Source: Constructed by the authors.

parent-child pairs was considered as a unit that contributed child variables and parental variables.

The two competing hypotheses represented by the correspondence model and the independence model were tested by subjecting all the variables except age (see later) to confirmatory factor analysis in order to compare the structural relationships between parent and child responses. Alpha factor analysis (Kaiser and Caffrey 1965) was used as the method of factor extraction. This method groups variables according to their common factor variance as computed by the widely used measure of internal consistency, coefficient α (Cronbach 1951). Alpha factoring is particularly relevant in the present case, as alpha was relied on in previous analyses of these data as a criterion for index construction (see especially Chapter 4).

The factors were then rotated according to the Quartimax criterion. This method tries to maximize the variance accounted for by each variable in the study, that is, each row of the factor matrix. All methods of orthogonal rotation produce essentially the same factor structure (Nunnally 1978); however, in accordance with the confirmatory (as opposed to exploratory) role in which factor analysis is employed in this study, Quartimax rotation was deliberately chosen over the more common Varimax method because of the tendency of Quartimax to try to load the variables on one large common factor. Note that this method provides maximal opportunity for the correspondence model to be confirmed. Failure to find correspondence would therefore signify clear rejection of this, the generally assumed parent-child influence model.

The rotated factor matrix for the total sample is shown in Table 7.3. Fifteen factors with eigenvalues greater than 1.0 were extracted from the 60 variables; eigenvalues less than 1.0 would signify factors with very low generalizability to other variables in the study. Of the 15 factors, only the first 6 individually accounted for over 5 percent of the variance in the correlation matrix and had α reliabilities larger than .70, and so only these are shown. Factor loadings above .30, indicating variables that account for at least 9 percent of the factor's variance, have been underlined to aid in factor interpretation.

The factor analytic results clearly allow rejection of the correspondence model as an explanation of parent-child influence. Children's dispositions toward proprietary drugs are entirely independent of parental dispositions, as are their illness patterns and proprietary drug usage patterns. Specifically, factor 1 is a general factor consisting of the child's global disposition toward proprietary medicines, that is, belief in their efficacy, affect toward taking them, intent to take them, and tendency to request proprietary

TABLE 7.3

Factor Matrix for the Total Sample (N = 612 Dyads)[a]

Variable	Factor					
	1	2	3	4	5	6

Child Variables

Colds						
Illness frequency	08	-02	13	<u>63</u>	-00	01
Belief	<u>40</u>	08	08	07	02	05
Affect	<u>66</u>	05	01	02	-04	-03
Intent	<u>69</u>	03	-02	08	-04	04
Requests	<u>56</u>	02	02	08	01	05
Usage	15	06	10	<u>55</u>	-08	08
Coughs						
Illness frequency	11	02	10	<u>58</u>	-01	00
Belief	<u>39</u>	07	-02	03	02	05
Affect	<u>66</u>	02	02	-03	-03	03
Intent	<u>75</u>	01	05	05	07	02
Requests	<u>70</u>	02	03	08	01	-05
Usage	12	13	18	<u>51</u>	-02	03
Headaches						
Illness frequency	12	-01	-12	<u>45</u>	-03	06
Belief	<u>31</u>	03	01	01	04	-01
Affect	<u>50</u>	03	-03	01	-01	03
Intent	<u>47</u>	02	-07	16	05	05
Requests	<u>51</u>	02	-04	11	-00	-03
Usage	02	-05	02	<u>52</u>	19	04
Stomachaches						
Illness frequency	16	05	-05	<u>44</u>	-06	-05
Belief	<u>44</u>	08	05	03	-00	09
Affect	<u>68</u>	05	05	-01	03	01
Intent	<u>67</u>	05	-02	15	01	04
Requests	<u>70</u>	04	-01	11	06	-01
Usage	28	08	00	<u>35</u>	-02	02

Parental Assessment of Child Variables

Colds						
Illness frequency	01	07	<u>68</u>	04	07	02
Requests	10	20	12	03	-01	04
Usage	05	24	<u>53</u>	08	04	13
Coughs						
Illness frequency	0i	09	<u>78</u>	07	05	06
Requests	04	17	16	03	11	01
Usage	01	21	<u>60</u>	11	03	04

Variable	Factor					
	1	2	3	4	5	6
Headaches						
Illness frequency	04	05	19	10	07	08
Requests	04	08	08	05	18	07
Usage	-01	09	<u>38</u>	20	<u>36</u>	04
Stomachaches						
Illness frequency	11	07·	24	05	01	16
Requests	12	15	05	05	-02	22
Usage	02	11	22	04	-01	<u>34</u>

Parental Variables

Variable	1	2	3	4	5	6
Colds						
Illness frequency	06	16	<u>54</u>	06	05	09
Belief	03	<u>60</u>	-03	-02	03	01
Affect	05	<u>58</u>	10	-01	06	05
Intent	07	<u>62</u>	09	03	09	08
Usage	05	<u>40</u>	21	04	01	08
Coughs						
Illness frequency	01	14	<u>50</u>	05	08	18
Belief	02	<u>61</u>	07	-03	15	04
Affect	02	<u>73</u>	13	02	14	09
Intent	04	<u>64</u>	09	09	10	00
Usage	06	<u>33</u>	21	03	-01	04
Headaches						
Illness frequency	06	02	10	-01	24	28
Belief	05	28	04	-01	<u>69</u>	-02
Affect	00	<u>34</u>	06	-02	<u>72</u>	01
Intent	-04	24	04	-02	<u>68</u>	-00
Usage	09	08	13	-03	<u>68</u>	15
Stomachaches						
Illness frequency	01	04	13	03	01	<u>58</u>
Belief	06	<u>50</u>	03	06	08	<u>43</u>
Affect	04	<u>39</u>	-03	01	05	<u>55</u>
Intent	05	<u>45</u>	00	00	09	<u>56</u>
Usage	-00	07	11	02	-01	<u>71</u>

Independent Variables

Variable	1	2	3	4	5	6
Parent-child mediation (C)[b]	26	-01	-01	<u>34</u>	-13	-00
Parent-child mediation (P)[c]	11	01	19	02	-04	14
Medicine advertising exposure	17	-00	-01	07	-08	-04

[a] Alpha-factored matrix with Quartimax rotation. Decimal points for the factor loadings have been omitted for greater clarity.

[b] Parent-child mediation as perceived by the child.

[c] Parent-child mediation as perceived by the parent.

Source: Compiled by the authors.

medicines when symptoms occur. The disposition is global in that there is no differentiation by type of illness. Note that parental dispositions have no influence (all loadings are less than .09) on children's dispositions.

Factor 2, which is, of course, orthogonal to (uncorrelated with) factor 1, picks up parental dispositions toward cold and cough remedies and also usage of these two categories of proprietary medicines. It also picks up parental dispositions toward stomach remedies but not, interestingly enough, headache remedies nor usage of either of these two categories. Headaches and stomach-aches are represented by two separate factors (5 and 6) for parents. Thus there are three parental factors in all: a cold and cough factor (factor 2), a headache factor (factor 5), and a stomachache factor (factor 6). This separation pattern is in marked contrast with the global structure for children.

Another major difference in addition to the failure of parent and child responses to correspond is that parental usage of pro-prietary medicines appears to be under attitudinal control, that is, based on need. For parents, usage loads highly on the dispositional factors; moreover, for colds, coughs, and headaches especially, parental usage of proprietary medicines is much more strongly based on dispositions than frequency of illness. The single excep-tion to this is for stomach remedies, where usage is aligned closely with stomach illness frequency as well as dispositions. For chil-dren, on the other hand, usage of proprietary medicines is only weakly related to dispositions but strongly related to illness fre-quency, as evidenced by the high loading of illness frequency and usage on a separate factor (factor 4) from the children's general disposition factor (factor 1). The separation of usage from disposi-tions in the case of children, of course, suggests the mediating role of parents in determining children's usage.

Surprisingly, however, children's reported usage and parental assessment of children's usage are unrelated. This is true also for children's reports versus parental assessment of illness frequency. Children's reports, as noted, comprise factor 6, whereas parental assessments tend to form a separate factor (factor 3) for colds and coughs or be split on smaller independent factors. It is possible that this was a rather difficult recall task for parents and children with regard to the illness and usage variables in that the respondents were asked to estimate how often each of the four symptom types had occurred and how often each type of proprietary medicine had been used in the previous six months. Thus perceptions of illness frequency and proprietary medicine usage may have been measured rather than actual behavior. If so, this would constitute further evidence for the independence model in that children's self-perceptions differ from the image presented to parents.

Interestingly, parents tend to recall that their children are less often ill and use proprietary medicines less frequently than the children themselves recall (Table 7.4). For all symptoms and proprietary medicine types, the parental assessments are substantially lower than the children's own reports; even the smallest difference, for headache remedy usage, is significant beyond the .001 level. In earlier research it was found that parents are subject to social desirability bias when reporting about their children's behavior, whereas children seem free of this tendency (Rossiter and Robertson, 1975). A similar phenomenon may have occurred in the present study. There seems to be little reason why children would exaggerate their illness frequency and usage (via parents) of proprietary medicines. The more likely explanation is that parents minimize the extent to which they perceive or recall their children being ill and using proprietary medicines, perhaps because this seems socially desirable.

Independent Variables

The factor analytic results in Table 7.3 strongly suggest that the independence model of parent-child influence in regard to proprietary medicines is the appropriate one. A question remains as to how the independent outcomes may have been reached. Some indication of the process underlying these outcomes is provided by the independent variables included in the study.

Parent-child mediation (as reported by children) appears to have a small but positive influence on children's dispositions toward proprietary medicines (a factor loading of $r = .26$ on factor 1) and on children's illness and usage (a factor loading of $r = .34$ on factor 4). In relying on children's reports of parent-child mediation, parents are actually given the benefit of the doubt, as their own reports of mediation have even lower loadings. Although the aforementioned loadings are highly significant ($p < .001$ in both cases), they suggest that parent-child mediation is no more than a small contributor to children's responses, accounting for 5 to 10 percent of the variance at most. The mean level of mediation is also fairly low: children reported about 9.5 discussions with parents about illness and proprietary medicines, on average, in the past six months, or about one and a half interactions per month. It may be noted from Table 7.4 that parents report even fewer interactions.

Overall, this pattern suggests that the third process identified in conjunction with the independence model is responsible for the independent outcome. A high contribution for parent-child mediation would have suggested the "do as I say, not as I do" process. A very

TABLE 7.4

Means and Standard Deviations for All Variables

	Child Variables		Parental Assessment of Child Variables		Parental Variables	
	Mean	Standard Deviation	Mean	Standard Deviation	Mean	Standard Deviation
Colds						
Illness frequency	3.3	1.5	2.3	1.2	1.9	1.8
Belief	3.3	.8	—[a]	—	3.0	1.0
Affect	2.4	1.0	—	—	2.1	1.2
Intent	2.5	1.0	—	—	1.9	.7
Requests	2.4	1.0	1.8	.8	—	—
Usage	2.7	1.8	1.8	1.7	1.4	1.7
Coughs						
Illness frequency	3.5	1.5	2.2	1.3	1.7	1.3
Belief	3.2	.8	—	—	2.8	1.1
Affect	2.5	1.0	—	—	2.4	1.2
Intent	2.5	1.0	—	—	2.0	.7
Requests	2.5	1.0	1.8	.8	—	—
Usage	2.6	1.9	1.9	1.7	1.3	1.7
Headaches						
Illness frequency	2.3	1.7	1.0	1.3	1.9	1.8
Belief	3.2	.8	—	—	3.1	1.1
Affect	2.8	1.0	—	—	2.7	1.3
Intent	2.5	1.0	—	—	2.2	.9
Requests	2.6	1.0	1.9	.9	—	—
Usage	3.2	1.8	2.8	1.8	2.4	2.0
Stomachaches						
Illness frequency	2.2	1.6	.7	1.1	.6	1.2
Belief	3.0	.9	—	—	2.3	1.1
Affect	2.5	1.0	—	—	1.6	1.0
Intent	2.2	1.1	—	—	1.6	.7
Requests	2.3	1.1	1.6	.7	—	—
Usage	1.4	1.7	.6	1.2	.6	1.4
Independent variables						
Parent-child mediation	9.5	6.5	—	—	7.5	6.5
Medicine advertising exposure	13.5	7.9	—	—	—	—

Note: Measurement details are as follows (see also Chapter 4): illness frequency figures and usage figures indicate the incidence of the illness and the number of times a proprietary medicine was administered over a six-month period; belief, affect, intent, and requests were measured on 1 to 4 scales, where 1 = lowest and 4 = highest; parent-child mediation figures, which ranged from 0 to a possible 25, refer to the number of parent-child discussions about illness and proprietary medicines over a six-month period; medicine advertising exposure figures indicate number of 30-second proprietary medicine commercials (potential exposure) per week.

[a]Means not measured.

Source: Compiled by the authors.

low or zero contribution would have suggested the "say nothing" process. The present results appear somewhere in between, suggesting that children listen to parents (and other sources) but form their own conclusions. The fact that parent-child mediation contributes positively to children's attitudes and usage while being unrelated to parents' attitudes and usage further suggests that discussions about illness and medicines serve moderately to increase the salience of these phenomena for children without imparting any degree of correspondence in parent and child viewpoints.

A second source of information, children's exposure to television advertising for proprietary medicines, reveals a small but significant relationship with children's dispositions (a factor loading of r = .17 on factor 1, p < .001). Inspection of the correlation matrix shows televised medicine advertising to have its highest effect on children's request tendencies, which is in accord with the findings reported in Chapter 5. Allowing for some unreliability (α = .73) in the measure, children's exposure to this advertising at most accounts for a further 10 percent of the variance in children's dispositions, with no discernible effect on usage, however.

All these data appear to leave children's own personal experience as the primary explanation of children's proprietary medicine attitudes and behavior. They may listen to or imitate parents somewhat, and pay some attention to medicine advertising on television, as well as to other sources, but it seems as if there is a large independent source of influence that reduces to the child's own experience with illness and proprietary medicines and his or her personal interpretation of their effectiveness and appropriateness.

Developmental Trends

To examine the child's experiential process further, three separate factor analyses were conducted by grade level as a cross-sectional simulation of developmental trends. In each case alpha factoring with Quartimax rotation was used, as before. These results are shown in Table 7.5. Only the factor loadings for the first factor emerging at each grade level are shown because, just as in the total sample results, parental responses loaded on the same cold-cough, headache, and stomachache factors found earlier. This finding alone, incidentally, provides strong support for the independence model in that children and their parents exhibit independent response patterns by the time the child is eight years old and continue to do so throughout the remainder of the childhood period.

TABLE 7.5

First-Factor Loadings by Grade Level[a]

Variable	Grade 3	Grade 5	Grade 7
Colds			
Illness frequency	11	-05	10
Belief	27	30	44
Affect	61	62	71
Intent	68	73	68
Requests	53	61	47
Usage	03	10	28
Coughs			
Illness frequency	10	03	12
Belief	22	38	36
Affect	60	75	61
Intent	70	77	75
Requests	69	68	64
Usage	06	06	19
Headaches[b]			
Illness frequency	12	23	-01
Belief	26	35	21
Affect	51	51	37
Intent	55	51	30
Requests	60	47	34
Usage	09	-01	03
Stomachaches			
Illness frequency	07	15	19
Belief	34	31	51
Affect	64	69	64
Intent	65	62	70
Requests	72	59	72
Usage	17	19	41
Independent variables			
Parent-child mediation	30	24	23
Medicine advertising exposure	17	15	15

[a]Factor extraction and rotation as in Table 7.3. Decimal points for factor loadings again omitted for clarity of presentation.

[b]As noted in text, by seventh grade the children's headache responses form a separate factor, hence the lower loadings on the general disposition factor.

Source: Compiled by the authors.

Two interesting trends are evident in the children's developmental sequence. First, although young children have very strong beliefs in the efficacy of proprietary medicines (see Figure 7.1), these beliefs do not become firmly aligned with the other components of attitude (affect and intent) until later childhood. Although headache remedy beliefs appear to be an exception to this pattern, the explanation is that by seventh grade the children's headache attitudes begin to separate from the global disposition factor and form a separate factor, exactly as in the parental pattern. Stomachache attitudes, however, do not separate, indicating that discrimination of stomachaches as a separate illness and proprietary medicine usage category may be a relatively late phenomenon in the learning sequence.

The second interesting trend is the increasing tendency for usage of proprietary medicines to coalesce with attitude rather than illness frequency as children grow older. Although this is not a strong trend, it does seem to indicate that an adult pattern is developing. It will be recalled that parental usage of proprietary medicines is largely under attitudinal rather than illness, that is, need-based, control.

The most informative result from the grade-level analysis, however, is that the trends toward a more adultlike pattern are still independent of the child's own parent's responses (full results would be too cumbersome to present here, but the parental loadings on children's factors remained uniformly low). Also, the significant but small influence of parent-child mediation and children's exposure to medicine advertising remain reasonably constant with increasing grade level. In summary, therefore, children appear to interpret their own experiences with proprietary medicines as the primary basis for emerging attitudes. These attitudes, in turn, increasingly tend to govern usage. This is in accord with Campbell's independence model (and represents a much broader validation of his findings) and quite contrary to the commonsense correspondence model of parent-child influence that is typically assumed.

CONCLUSIONS

The conclusions suggest that, although children become more adultlike with age and experience in their conceptions and usage of proprietary medicines, this process is not attributable to parental influence. Rather, children appear to learn more discriminating and more moderate attitudes toward these products by interpreting their own usage experiences—largely independently of what parents tell them and largely independently of media influence. This conclusion is in accord with recent studies of socialization (Skolnick 1978) and child development (Gelman 1978), which conclude that the influential role of the parent has been overestimated and the independent ability of the child underestimated.

Several possible counterarguments to this conclusion need to be addressed. Although the results indicate that independent attitudes are established by age 8, it is possible that the attitudes of younger children may correspond more closely with those of their parents. If so, these attitudes certainly change dramatically by middle childhood.

A further counterargument is that it is possible that the measures of usage, which are based on recalled usage over a substantial period, reflect to some extent perceived usage rather than actual usage. Direct observational studies could reveal greater correspondence between actual frequencies of parent and child proprietary medicine usage than the results indicate. The illness frequency or "need" measures are also subject to limitations of recall. However, it would still remain to be answered why parents' and children's dispositions (that is, attitudes) toward proprietary drugs are intrafamilially independent, as the disposition measures do not involve recall. A constructive direction for further research might be to examine whether these dispositions indeed serve to control proprietary medicine usage to a greater extent than illness frequency, as the findings imply, when the latter two variables are more concretely measured.

It is also possible that fathers' responses may show greater correspondence with children's responses than did those of mothers, who served as the parental reporters in the study. Given the prior evidence on the dominant role of mothers as the family consultant for illness and its treatment, however, this possibility seems remote.

Finally, the use of self-administered questionnaires with children and telephone interviews with parents (see Chapter 4) might have contributed to the independence of the parent-child outcomes through some hard to define methodological factor. In this connection it should be recalled that the correspondence model was given the best possible chance to emerge in the factor analysis by using Quartimax factor rotation. It is tempting to conclude that any differences due to methodology would be offset by the similarities conferred by the analysis.

What broader implications may be drawn from the findings? There are two major ones. One concerns the obvious question: If parents have little direct influence on children's conceptions and usage of proprietary medicines, then who does? The answer seems to be, children themselves. Children, under their own reconnaissance, appear to form quite discriminating and moderate attitudes toward these products; they become adultlike in their own way.

The other implication pertains to parents who desire to exert more control over children's illness and medication attitudes than they may be achieving now. The results would caution parents that frequent discussion about illness and proprietary medicines may only serve to increase the positive direction of children's attitudes by making these aspects of the child's life more salient. Children's attitudes toward proprietary medicines may also be inadvertently reinforced by parents who, in order to facilitate the child's medicine taking, describe these remedies as being particularly effective. Certainly more precise knowledge of the content and dynamics of the parental influence process is needed.

It is important to note, however, that knowledge of the process of parent-child communication would in no way alter the independent outcome observed in the analysis. In fact, it is urged that future research be addressed not only to the question of effective parent-child communication but also to the question of how children become such effective learners in their own right about illness and proprietary medicine use.

REFERENCES

Alpert, Joel J., John Kosa, and Robert J. Haggerty. 1967. "A Month of Illness and Health Care Among Low-Income Families." Public Health Reports 82 (August): 705-13.

Campbell, John D. 1975. "Illness Is a Point of View: The Development of Children's Concepts of Illness." Child Development 46 (March): 92-100.

Cronbach, Lee J. 1951. "Coefficient Alpha and the Internal Structure of Tests." Psychometrika 16 (September): 297-334.

Gelman, Rochel. 1978. "Cognitive Developments." In Annual Review of Psychology, edited by Mark R. Rosenzweig and Lyman W. Porter, vol. 29, pp. 297-332. Palo Alto, Calif.: Annual Reviews.

Kaiser, Henry F., and John Caffrey. 1965. "Alpha Factor Analysis." Psychometrika 30 (March): 1-14.

Knapp, D. A., D. E. Knapp, and J. Engle. 1966. "The Public, the Pharmacist, and Self-Medication." Journal of the American Pharmaceutical Association 56 (September): 460-62.

Litman, Theodor J. 1974. "The Family as a Basic Unit in Health and Medical Care: A Social-Behavioral Overview." Social Science and Medicine 8 (September): 495-519.

_____. 1971. "Health Care and the Family: A Three-Generational Analysis." Medical Care 9 (January-February): 67-81.

Nunnally, Jum C. 1978. Psychometric Theory. 2nd ed. New York: McGraw-Hill.

Richardson, William C. 1970. "Measuring the Urban Poor's Use of Physician's Services in Response to Illness Episodes." Medical Care 8 (March-April): 132-42.

Rossiter, John R., and Thomas S. Robertson. 1975. "Children's Television Viewing: An Examination of Parent-Child Consensus." Sociometry 38 (September) 308-26.

Skolnick, Arlene. 1978. "The Myth of the Vulnerable Child." Psychology Today, February 1978, pp. 56, 58, 60, 65.

Target Group Index. 1975. Miscellaneous Drug Products. Report P-20. New York: Axiom Market Research Bureau.

8

AN EMPIRICAL MODEL

In this chapter some evidence is presented for a model of the structure among variables describing children's attitudes and behavior toward proprietary medicines. The approach is to use the tools of regression analysis to investigate an elaborated form of the hierarchy-of-effects model (Lavidge and Steiner 1961; Ray et al. 1973; Fishbein and Ajzen 1975). Because the model may be stated in the form of a set of recursive equations, ordinary least squares computations permit estimation of the effects of various influences on attitudinal and usage patterns concerning proprietary medicines. Although the analysis is complex, and the results complicated by the use of moderating variables to describe the nature of various effects, the use of simulation employing coefficients estimated for the model from survey data permits the graphic portrayal of the dependence of beliefs, attitudes, and usage variables on several important factors, including exposure to television advertising.

STRUCTURE OF THE MODEL

Endogenous Variables

The structure of variable relationships appears as a kind of skeleton whose backbone is the hierarchy-of-effects model illustrated in Figure 8.1. The structure begins with belief in the efficacy of medicines (belief) (see Chapter 4 for a detailed description of the measurement of this and the following variables) as the first step in a chain of effects leading to usage of such medicines. The conjecture is that if children believe that medicines can make them feel better, then they will come to have a positive affect for taking medicines (affect). Positive increases in affect should lead to positive increases in intention to take medicines (intent) the next time the child is sick. With positive intention, the child should increase the frequency of requests for medicine (requests) when sick. Requests in turn should contribute to actual use of proprietary medicines (usage).

FIGURE 8.1

Basic Hierarchy-of-Effects Model

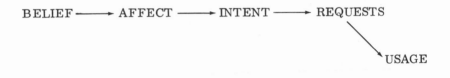

Source: Constructed by the authors.

The model proposes a set of effects that follows a causal sequence. Unfortunately, the time series data necessary for making a direct test of this sequence are not available. Rather, cross-sectional data from the survey must be used to search for indirect support for the model. Thus, whether those respondents high on the belief variable tend also to be high on the affect variable, and so forth, must be examined.

The pattern of causal effects is straightforward with the possible exception that the contribution of requests to usage is undoubtedly attenuated by numerous other effects. Although children may want and ask to take medicines, in most families the actual administration of medicines is controlled by parents. The decisions that lead to usage stem from numerous variables that are not part of the influences that might reasonably be expected to determine the attitudinal and behavior variables belief, affect, intent, and requests. Thus, the requests-usage relationship will require special attention. The unique status of the usage variable has been symbolized by placing it on a different line from the other variables in Figure 8.1.

Exogenous Variables

The endogenous variables of Figure 8.1 are the primary outcome variables of interest in this study. However, they are insufficient as an explanation of usage behavior. Consequently, one can conjecture that the following variables have significant relationships to the endogenous variables:

Parental Variables

In parallel with each of the children's variables, the corresponding measures for parents are available. Thus there is parental belief in the efficacy of proprietary medicines (parent-belief), parental affect toward taking medicines (parent-affect), parental intention to take medicines (parent-usage). (Obviously, there is no parental counterpart to the requests variable.) The supposition is that each of these variables should be positively related to the corresponding variable for children. Thus, for example, those parents who have a strong positive belief about the efficacy of proprietary medicines should communicate that belief to their children. Because children tend to identify with their parents, they, too, should have positive values for the belief variable. Similarly, parents who often use proprietary medicines should frequently administer such medicines to their children.

Illness Experience (ILLEXP)

Children who are frequently ill have ample opportunity to experience relief as a result of taking proprietary medicines. Hence they are apt to have more positive beliefs, affect, intent, and request scores than children who are infrequently ill. Likewise, children who report often being ill should also report high levels of usage.

Exposure to Advertising (ADEXP)

One of the central variables in this study is children's exposure to proprietary medicine advertising. It is conjectured that this variable should have positive effects at all stages of the hierarchy—belief, affect, intent, requests—except for usage. Although it seems reasonable that advertising should function to increase awareness, promote positive feelings, and stimulate people to action, it is not so clear that television advertising should stimulate usage directly. Thus the translation of requests into usage is a social rather than attitudinal process. Because ADEXP should work only on the attitudinal states of the respondents, ADEXP was not included in the equation for usage.

Parental Control of Medicine Usage (PCMU)

The request and usage equations need special treatment. In addition to those variables listed above, the requests equation is posited to include a measure of the extent to which parents exercise control over the administration of proprietary medicines (elsewhere in this book the reverse of the PCMU variable has been called self-administration). The notion is that the more control exercised by parents, the more necessary requests are. Conversely, requests are unnecessary if the child is permitted to take proprietary medicines on his or her own.

Specific Mediation (SM)

This variable, which is intended to measure the extent to which parents talk to their children about proprietary medicines and when to take them, was included as an explanatory variable for the usage equation. The conjecture was that children who discuss proprietary medicines with their parents should acquire, in the process, a discriminating view of the appropriateness and utility of these medicines. As a consequence, reports of frequent conversations, that is, high levels of specific mediation (SM), should be associated with low levels of usage. All of the above relationships are summarized in Figure 8.2. Each arrow between two variables indicates that the variable at the tail of the arrow contributes to the equation of the variable at the head of the arrow. The set of all those arrows that terminate at a variable denotes the explanatory variables that enter into its equation.

Moderator Variables

Figure 8.2 does not represent the final specification of the model. Indeed, it is reasonable to suppose that there exist variables that should influence the strength of the relationship between exogenous and endogenous variables. For example, one might postulate that the correlation between belief and parent-belief should diminish over time as children come to depend less on their parents for their view of the world and to use other information sources, including their own experience. Consequently, grade in school, used as a surrogate for development in the child, may be said to moderate the relationship between belief and parent-belief.

The following procedure has been adopted for incorporating moderator variables within a regression framework. Let Y be an endogenous (outcome) variable, X an exogenous (explanatory) variable, and M a moderating variable. Then, if the basic model relating X and Y is

$$Y = b_0 + b_1 X + e_1 \tag{8.1}$$

FIGURE 8.2

Expanded Model Including Exogenous Variables

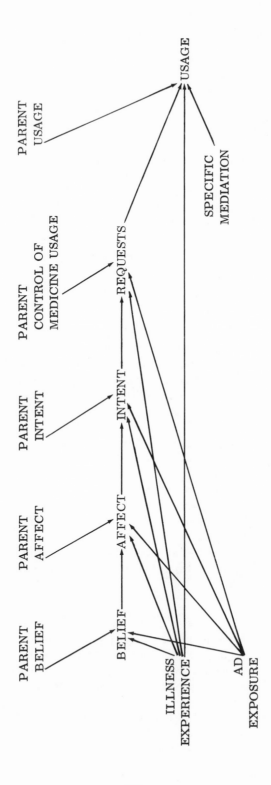

Source: Constructed by the authors.

107

(e_1 is an error term), then the moderating variable M is conceived as affecting the coefficient b_1, which controls the strength of the correlation between X and Y, that is

$$b_1 = a_0 + a_1 M + e_2 \qquad (8.2)$$

Equation 8.2 is the definitional form for what is referred to as a moderating variable in this chapter. It is a strong form of the moderating variable notion inasmuch as the correlation between X and Y is posited to be a linear function of the variable M. Moreover, this usage of M is more powerful than the common practice of dichotomizing M at its median and running separate regressions for the two subsamples so formed because it takes advantage of all the information available in M.

Substituting Equation 8.2 into Equation 8.1 yields

$$Y = b_0 + a_0 X + a_1 XM + (e_2 X + e_1) \qquad (8.3)$$

This equation is in the standard form for ordinary least squares regression in which the essential features of the moderating effect of M are captured by the product term XM. If, in the estimation of the coefficients b_0, a_0, and a_1, it turns out that a_1 is significantly different from zero, then M is truly moderating the relationship between X and Y.

The whole argument from Equation 8.1 to Equation 8.3 may be straightforwardly generalized to accommodate more variables. In the discussion below, it will be seen that models corresponding to both of these equations will have more than one explanatory variable. Such an extension poses no serious problems. It simply means that the regression equations will consist of several product terms and will be more complex to interpret, but otherwise these changes entail no new ideas. With the addition of these analytic tools, it is now possible to consider several potential moderating variables.

Grade

It has been conjectured that grade may act as a moderating variable on every one of the relationships of exogenous variables to the endogenous variables of belief, affect, intent, and requests. In particular, the expectation is that, because children as they get older become less dependent on their parents for attitudes, grade should reduce the effect of the parent variables (for example, parent-affect) on the corresponding child variables. Because of increased cognitive abilities with increasing age, grade should increase the effect of ILLEXP on belief, affect, intent, and requests, but it should reduce the relationship of television advertising (ADEXP) on these same variables.

Illness Anxiety (ILLANX)

The more anxious a child is about illness, the more sensitive he or she should be to attitude-forming influences. Thus ILLANX should work to enhance the relationship of the parental variables, illness experience, and ad exposure to belief, affect, intent, and requests.

Specific Mediation (SM)

The original conjecture was that specific mediation, that is, the extent to which parents discuss proprietary medicines and medicine commercials with their children, should work to reduce the influence of the exogenous variables on the endogenous variables. (The expectation was that the enhanced discrimination that should arise from discussions with parents would lessen the influence of ILLEXP, ADEXP, and the parental variables. In fact, as will be seen from the results discussed below, this conjecture is quite wrong.)

Parents as an Information Source (PINF)

If a child reports that parents are a source of information about medicines, then it should follow that the same child should be more sensitive to the views of his or her parents. Consequently, PINF should moderate, positively, the relationship between the parental variables and the corresponding variables for the children.

Parental Control of Medicine Usage (PCMU)

This variable was hypothesized to be a major link in the relationship between requests, ILLEXP, SM, parent-usage, and the endogenous usage variables. In each case, whether or not the exogenous influence gets translated into child usage ought to depend on the extent to which parents are serving as a mediator of proprietary medicines.

RESULTS

The preceding discussion describes a recursive model with five equations, one for each of the endogenous variables. (Note that variables that are endogenous in some equations may be exogenous

in others, for example, affect is used as an explanatory variable in
the intent equation. The endogenous-exogenous terminology has
been employed here to distinguish those variables in the core of the
model, and therefore sometimes appearing as endogenous variables,
from those that are always used as explanatory variables.) The results of estimating the coefficients for these equations are given in
Tables 8.1 to 8.5. The coefficients in each table indicate the weight
given to the corresponding term in the reduced version of the model
(that is, the form comparable to Equation 8.3). Wherever a moderating variable occurs in the table (denoted by an asterisk), the ac-
companying coefficient is to be interpreted as applying to the product
term composed of the moderating variable and the exogenous variable
given above it. Because the coefficients are influenced by the units
used to measure both the independent and dependent variables, the
column labeled "standard error" can be used as a rough indication
of the relative sizes of the effects contributed by each independent
variable. The column of each table labeled "p" gives the significance level for the test of the hypothesis that the corresponding coefficient does not differ from zero.

Interpreting a moderating variable equation is a little more
difficult than the ordinary regression equation. Although the effects
of the moderating variable may be read clearly enough from the
signs and magnitudes of the coefficients of the product terms, the
effects of the exogenous variables are less clear. For example, in
Table 8.1, grade appears to enhance the relationship between parent-
belief and belief (contrary to a priori expectations), whereas ILLANX,
SM, and PINF all tend to reduce the relationship. Moreover, judging
from the standard errors of the variables, a one-standard-deviation
change in grade or PINF will have a comparatively greater effect on
the relationship than would similar changes in ILLANX or SM. But
the actual nature of the correlation is less clear, inasmuch as the
-.174 given as the coefficient for parent-belief describes only the
effect of this variable when all the moderator variables take on the
value of zero, which, of course, never happens. Moreover, because several of the variables were scored with negative values (to
make changes in the variables consistent with the substantive label
for the variable), the actual contribution of a moderating variable to
the relationship is somewhat obscured.

In order to assist, therefore, in the interpretation of the relationships between exogenous and endogenous variables, two more
columns appear in each table. The column headed "Average Contribution" gives the product of the mean of the moderating variable and
the corresponding coefficient for that product term. Thus, in Table
8.1, ILLANX contributes .0255 on the average to the coefficient
governing the relationship between parent-belief and belief. As

TABLE 8.1

Coefficients for Empirical Model of Belief

Variables	Coefficient	Standard Error	p	Average Coefficient[a]	Average Contribution[b]
Parental belief	-.174	.118	ns[c]	.107	.175
*Grade	.0348	.0137	<.05		.0255
*Illness anxiety	-.000984	.00329	ns		-.0231
*Specific mediation	-.00119	.00171	ns		.103
*Parents as an information source	-.0585	.0117	<.01		
Illness experience	.133	.0866	ns	.0123	-.123
*Grade	-.0244	.0105	<.05		.000317
*Illness anxiety	-.0000122	.00241	ns		.00168
*Specific mediation	.0000865	.00126	ns		
Ad exposure	.108	.0819	ns	.0361	.0709
*Grade	.0141	.0102	ns		-.126
*Illness anxiety	.00487	.00238	<.05		-.0164
*Specific mediation	-.000844	.00120	ns		
(Constant)	-17.2				

R^2

Full model	.223				
Without ADEXP variables	.213				
Increment due to ADEXP variables	.010		<.10		

*Moderating variable.
[a]This is the coefficient obtained when all moderating variables are set at their mean.
[b]This is the contribution to the coefficient of the exogenous variable by the moderating variable when it is at its own mean.
[c]Not significant.
Source: Compiled by the authors.

111

TABLE 8.2

Coefficients for Empirical Model of Affect

Variables	Coefficient	Standard Error	p	Average Coefficient[a]	Average Contribution[b]
Belief	.595	.0466	<.01	.595	
Parent affect	-.0744	.118	ns[c]	.0103	-.0850
*Grade	-.0169	.0140	ns		.0984
*Illness anxiety	-.00379	.00339	ns		.0231
*Specific mediation	.00187	.00176	ns		.0482
*Parents as an information source	-.0273	.0110	<.05		
Illness experience	-.121	.107	ns	.0472	.0461
*Grade	.00917	.0131	ns		.104
*Illness anxiety	-.00399	.00304	ns		.0185
*Specific mediation	.000951	.000157	ns		
Ad Exposure	.271	.0968	<.01	-.0124	-.160
*Grade	-.0318	.0123	<.01		-.157
*Illness anxiety	.00605	.00283	<.05		.0336
*Specific mediation	.00173	.00142	ns		
(Constant)	-14.2				
R^2					
Full model	.338				
Without ADEXP variables	.317				
Increment due to ADEXP variables	.021		<.01		

*Moderating variable.

[a] This is the coefficient obtained when all moderating variables are set at their mean.

[b] This is the contribution to the coefficient of the exogenous variable by the moderating variable when it is at its own mean.

[c] Not significant.

Source: Compiled by the authors.

112

TABLE 8.3

Coefficients for Empirical Model of Intent

Variables	Coefficient	Standard Error	p	Average Coefficient[a]	Average Contribution[b]
Affect	.587	.0309	<.01	.587	
Parent intent	-.0268	.170	ns[c]	.0682	
*Grade	.0180	.0183	ns		.0905
*Illness anxiety	-.000193	.00465	ns		.00501
*Specific mediation	-.000235	.00252	ns		.0457
*Parents as an information source	.0262	.0145	<.10		-.0462
Illness experience	.182	.101	<.10	.0949	
*Grade	-.0127	.0122	ns		-.0639
*Illness anxiety	-.000307	.00283	ns		-.00797
*Specific mediation	-.000783	.00149	ns		-.0152
Ad exposure	-.0142	.0858	ns	.0201	
*Grade	-.00665	.0105	ns		-.0334
*Illness anxiety	-.00162	.00251	ns		.0420
*Specific mediation	.00132	.00123	ns		.0257
(Constant)	34.4				
R^2					
Full model	.466				
Without ADEXP variables	.463				
Increment due to ADEXP variables	.003		ns		

*Moderating variable.

[a] This is the coefficient obtained when all moderating variables are set at their mean.

[b] This is the contribution to the coefficient of the exogenous variable by the moderating variable when it is at its own mean.

[c] Not significant.

Source: Compiled by the authors.

TABLE 8.4

Coefficients for Empirical Model of Requests

Variables	Coefficient	Standard Error	p	Average Coefficient[a]	Average Contribution[b]
Intent	.633	.0297	<.01	.663	
Parental control of medicine usage	-.345	.175	<.05	.110	.430
*Grade	.0854	.0199	<.01		.00229
*Illness anxiety	-.0000881	.00448	ns[c]		
*Specific mediation	.00117	.00235	ns		.0227
Illness experience	-.0860	.0824	ns	.0218	
*Grade	.0188	.0102	<.10		.0946
*Illness anxiety	-.0000196	.00230	ns		.000509
*Specific mediation	.000656	.00122	ns		.0128
Ad exposure	-.0575	.0799	ns	.051	
*Grade	.0137	.00990	ns		.0689
*Illness anxiety	-.0000151	.00232	ns		.000392
*Specific mediation	.00202	.00114	<.10		.0393
(Constant)	8.61				

R^2			
Full model	.549		
Without ADEXP variables	.540		
Increment due to ADEXP variables	.009	<.05	

*Moderating variable.

[a]This is the coefficient obtained when all moderating variables are set at their mean.

[b]This is the contribution to the coefficient of the exogenous variable by the moderating variable when it is at its own mean.

[c]Not significant.

Source: Compiled by the authors.

114

TABLE 8.5

Coefficients for Empirical Model of Usage

Variables	Coefficient	Standard Error	p	Average Coefficient[a]	Average Contribution[b]
Requests	.141	.108	ns[c]	.116	
*Medicine control	.00178	.00681	ns		-.0254
Illness experience	.528	.0807	<.01	.452	
*Medicine control	.00533	.00503	ns		-.0759
Specific mediation	-.0360	.0790	ns	.188	
*Medicine control	-.0154	.00488	<.01		.224
Parent usage	.204	.0821	<.05	.146	
*Medicine control	.00406	.00505	ns		-.0578
(Constant)	3.80				

R^2

Full model .158

*Moderating variable.

[a]This is the coefficient obtained when all moderating variables are set at their mean.

[b]This is the contribution to the coefficient of the exogenous variable by the moderating variable when it is at its own mean.

[c]Not significant.

Source: Compiled by the authors.

ILLANX varies about its mean, its contribution will increase or decrease about the value .0255. In this particular case, increases in ILLANX will lead to decreases in the contribution of parent-belief to belief.

The column headed "Average Coefficient" gives the sum of all the contributions from the moderating variables (as well as the coefficient for the exogenous variable by itself). This, then, is the coefficient governing the relationship between the exogenous and endogenous variables that is observed on the average and that increases or decreases as the moderating variables change their values. In the discussion that follows, these two statistics will be referred to as average contribution and average coefficient. They are to be distinguished carefully from the ordinary regression coefficients that often have different signs as well as magnitudes.

Belief

As can be seen from the bottom of Table 8.1, the R^2 for the belief equation is only .223. Except for the usage equation, this is the lowest proportion of variance explained among the endogenous variables. To the extent that variance is explained by the exogenous variables for this equation, parent-belief, ILLEXP, and ADEXP all have positive average coefficients. Among the moderating variables, only a few seem to have very substantial effects. Grade appears to enhance the effect of parent-belief while reducing the contribution of ILLEXP, both somewhat unexpected findings. Reliance on parents as an information source (PINF) reduces the effect of parent-belief. On the other hand, increases in illness anxiety (ILLANX) appear to enhance the effects of ad exposure (ADEXP) on belief.

Affect

This model is on a somewhat firmer footing than the belief model, with an R^2 of .338, the dominant share of which is contributed by belief. Parent-affect, ILLEXP, and ADEXP all appear to have rather weak average coefficients with affect. However, rather sizable changes in the ADEXP coefficient are introduced by changes in grade and illness anxiety (ILLANX), the former negatively and the latter positively. Once again, PINF tends to reduce the relationship between the parental variable and its counterpart for the children.

Intent

In its general features, the model for intent is virtually the same as the model for affect. The R^2, .466, is higher than for the previous equation, an effect due primarily to the higher correlation between affect and intent than between belief and affect. The exogenous variables all have positive average coefficients. All the moderating variables seem to have negligible effects with the possible exception of PINF, which now contributes positively to the relationship between parent-intent and intent.

Requests

This model has the highest R^2 of all, .549. Once again the size of the R^2 is due primarily to an increased correlation between the preceding and the current endogenous variables. The exogenous variables all have positive average coefficients with requests. Grade appears to enhance substantially the relationship between parental control of medicine usage (PCMU) and requests while having a similar, but apparently smaller, effect on the contribution of illness experience. Specific mediation (SM) appears to increase the effectiveness of advertising (ADEXP) in directly stimulating requests.

Usage

The usage model, with an R^2 of .158, is the weakest of the five equations, primarily because requests is not a strong contributor to the explanation of usage. All of the exogenous variables in this equation have positive, albeit small, average coefficients. Interestingly, parental control of medicine usage (PCMU) has differing effects as a moderating variable; it makes small positive contributions to the correlations of requests, ILLEXP, and parent-usage with usage, but appears to make a fairly substantial negative contribution to the effects of specific mediation (SM).

DISCUSSION

At the very least, the pattern of results in Tables 8.1 through 8.5 is complex. Examining individual variable effects piecemeal tends to obscure the overall pattern of relationships in the data. As always, in this kind of analysis, one wants to know what the overall effects of various variables are. In particular, the contribution of exposure to advertising of proprietary medicines has been a central interest of this study.

There are two ways to approach the problem of putting the effects of ad exposure in context. The first is to observe the incremental contribution of the ADEXP variable and its associated moderating variables to the R^2 of each model. As can be seen from Tables 8.1 to 8.4, the incremental R^2 averages just over .01, which is a small effect indeed. But this is a very conservative test. The pattern of correlations among the exogenous variables undoubtedly obscures the full effect of ADEXP on the various outcome variables. In order to get at these effects more graphically, the coefficients estimated in Tables 8.1 to 8.5 can be used to simulate the effects of changes in certain specifically chosen variables.

It was decided to investigate the relative effects of ADEXP, parent-belief, and grade: the first because it was of primary interest in the study, the second because it would serve as a useful contrast to assess the size of the effects of ADEXP, and the latter because inspection of the regression results seemed to suggest that grade was the most persistently effective moderating variable.

A straightforward approach to investigating the implications of Tables 8.1 to 8.5 would be to set all exogenous variables, except the three singled out for examination, at their means and then calculate values for the endogenous variables as a function of specific values for ADEXP, parent-belief, and grade. Such a procedure works well enough, but it gives a rather artificial picture of the way the data are actually structured. Instead, additional equations were calculated—all of minor interest to the overall investigation—that would help take account of the fact that many of the exogenous variables are correlated.

Suppose, for example, that grade and PCMU (parental control of medicine usage) are correlated. Then setting PCMU at its mean and varying grade would underrepresent the actual changes in the data. Therefore, to capture the fact that PCMU is related to grade, the regression of PCMU onto grade should be added to the model. In particular, the following equations for illness experience, illness anxiety, specific mediation, and parental control of medicine usage were added:

$$\text{ILLEXP} = 34.53 - 1.221\text{grade} \qquad (8.4)$$

$$\text{ILLANX} = -21.8 - .9318 \text{ grade} + .0807\text{ILLEXP} \\ + .128(\text{parent-ILLANX}) + .07281(\text{parent-} \\ \text{ILLEXP}) - .07037(\text{parent-belief}) \qquad (8.5)$$

$$\text{SM} = 34.86 - .7671\text{grade} + .3704(\text{parent-} \\ \text{ILLANX}) - .0906(\text{parent-belief}) \qquad (8.6)$$

$$\text{PCMU} = -7.749 - 1.284\text{grade} \tag{8.7}$$

In addition to these equations, which govern variables describing the children's behavior, three equations were added to parallel for the parents the hierarchy-of-effects sequence demonstrated for the children. The following equations describe those effects (note that each variable name should be prefixed by parent-):

$$\text{affect} = -10.87 + .7849\text{belief} \tag{8.8}$$

$$\text{intent} = 32.24 + .2314\text{belief} + .277\text{affect} \tag{8.9}$$

$$\text{usage} = 8.274 + .7503\text{intent} + .2955\text{affect} \tag{8.10}$$

With the addition of Equations 8.4 to 8.10, it is now possible to simulate fairly completely the implications of Tables 8.1 to 8.5 with only three variables—PINF, parent-ILLEXP, and parent-ILLANX—set at their means. The results of these simulations appear in Figures 8.3 to 8.6. In calculating values for these figures, the high value of parent-belief was chosen at one standard deviation above its mean and the low value at one standard deviation below its mean. Similarly, the three values listed on the abscissa for ADEXP in each figure are the mean plus and minus one standard deviation. Grade, of course, simply reflects the three values observed in the data. The units for these figures are expressed in two ways to ease their interpretation. The raw scores are the units used in Tables 8.1 to 8.5 and Equations 8.4 to 8.10. The scale scores given along each ordinate are conversions of the units of the endogenous variables into their original response scale range (1–4 for belief, affect, intent, and requests; 0–5 for usage). Along each abscissa the ad exposure variable is also given in terms of ads per week.

The results in all these figures are quite striking. Ad exposure seems to influence belief only for older children and, even there, the positive slope of the lines is small. Even for the seventh graders, however, the changes in exposure to proprietary medicine ads seem to be much less effective than comparable changes in parent-belief. In Figure 8.4, the picture is quite different. Here ad exposure seems to have comparatively large effects on affect and these effects are in opposite directions for third and seventh graders. It appears that as children get older, television advertising is moving them from a positive feeling for proprietary medicines to a substantially negative position. Moreover, these effects overshadow differences due to parental beliefs (and, indirectly, parental affect).

FIGURE 8.3

Belief as a Function of ADEXP, Parent-Belief, and Grade

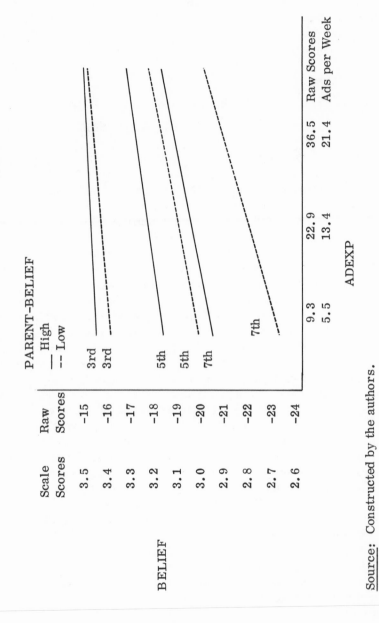

Source: Constructed by the authors.

FIGURE 8.4

Affect as a Function of ADEXP, Parent-Belief, and Grade

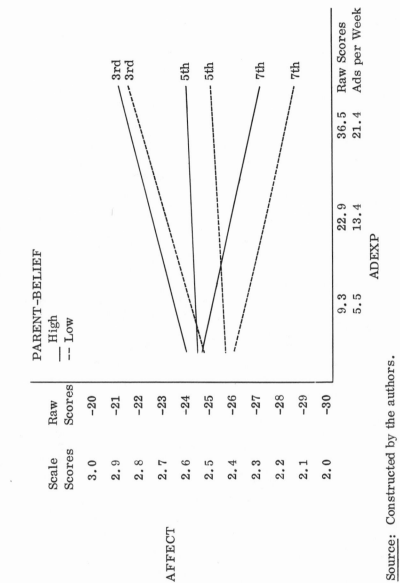

Source: Constructed by the authors.

121

FIGURE 8.5

Intent as a Function of ADEXP, Parent-Belief, and Grade

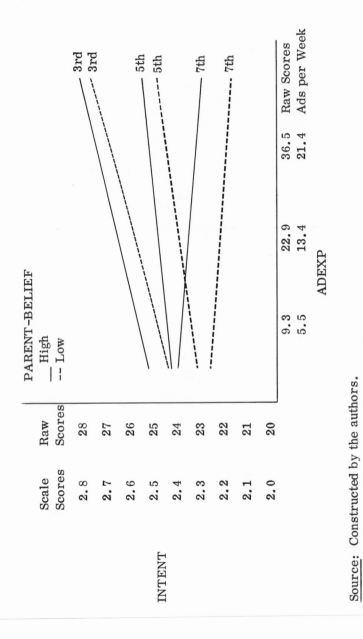

Source: Constructed by the authors.

FIGURE 8.6

Requests as a Function of ADEXP, Parent-Belief, and Grade

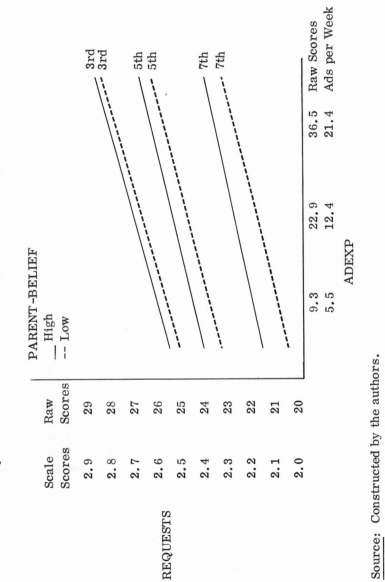

Source: Constructed by the authors.

123

The graphs for intent in Figure 8.5 are essentially the same as those for affect in Figure 8.4, with the exception that the negative effects of advertising on seventh graders are less pronounced. Figure 8.6 shows that the situation for requests is quite different. Ad exposure, through all of its indirect effects, has a positive effect on requests at all grade levels. Changes due to parental beliefs are comparatively small in contrast. But, even though there is a positive response to advertising, the developmental process revealed in the changes from one grade level to the next appears to be the dominant effect. Finally, Figure 8.7 reveals that advertising has apparently no effect on usage. Grade and parent-belief contribute something to the explanation of usage but on the whole, as Table 8.5 indicated, the model for describing usage is not yet very well developed.

A possibly troublesome aspect of this model as it has been developed is the question of why ad exposure has the effects it does. Conceivably, television viewing alone could equally well account for the effects encountered in Tables 8.1 to 8.4 and the simulation of Figures 8.3 to 8.7. Such an event would suggest that it is not exposure to proprietary medicine ads as such that is contributing to the endogenous variables, but something in the process that leads to television viewing itself. Yet another argument may be proffered that it is neither television viewing nor exposure to proprietary medicine ads that is the source of these effects, but rather some other variable, call it X, that is present in the family environment of the child. Thus, television exposure (TVEXP) and ADEXP would be the result of variation in X, and their covariation with the endogenous variables would be an incidental consequence of the fact that TVEXP, ADEXP, and the endogenous variables all have the same cause.

Unfortunately the data do not permit a complete unraveling of these competing explanations. There is, however, some evidence for the differential plausibility of each argument. Consider the causal model implied by Figure 8.8. If X is a sufficient cause of the variation in both the exposure variables and the endogenous variable, then in any equation intended to explain variation in the endogenous variable, X should contribute significantly, but TVEXP and ADEXP should not. Likewise, if ADEXP has no independent contribution to an endogenous variable, apart from mere exposure to television itself, then ADEXP should not make a significant contribution to any equation in which TVEXP is already employed as an explanatory variable. If, however, in either of these circumstances the exposure variables make significant contributions to the explanation of the endogenous variable in the presence of X (and TVEXP for ADEXP), then there is evidence for their independent status as causal variables.

FIGURE 8.7

Usage as a Function of ADEXP, Parent-Belief, and Grade

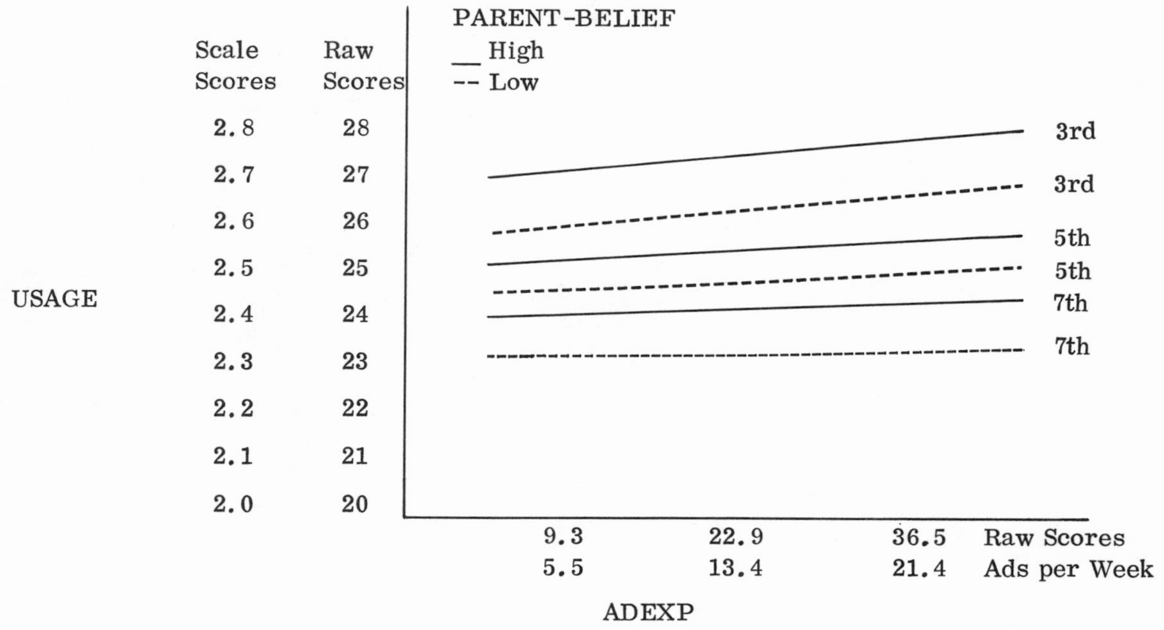

Source: Constructed by the authors.

125

FIGURE 8.8

Hypothetical Relationships among an Unknown Prior Cause X,
TVEXP, ADEXP, and Any One of the Endogenous Variables

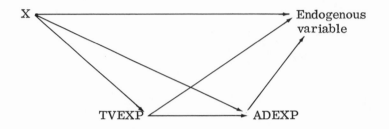

Source: Constructed by the authors.

Of course X is unknown. But a rough idea of how X might operate can be obtained from examining those variables that are
plausible surrogates for X and that explain variation in TVEXP.
Table 8.6 gives the coefficients and related statistics for those variables that significantly relate to children's television viewing. This
is the best equation that could be developed and may, therefore, represent capitalization on chance to some extent. Even so, the proportion of variance accounted for is not large, being comparable to
the value obtained for the belief equation (Table 8.1). For the following argument the linear combination of variables indicated in
Table 8.6 will be used as the unknown variable X.

Table 8.7 shows the pattern of variance accounted for in each
of the endogenous variables by X, TVEXP in the context of X, and
ADEXP in the context of X and TVEXP. Note that most of the names
given in this table represent not single variables, but classes of
variables consisting of an exogenous variable and product variables
involving it and several moderating variables in the same pattern
that was used in Tables 8.1 to 8.4. The results are quite consistent. X appears as a significant contributor in the belief, affect,
and requests equations. TVEXP appears as a significant contributor in the belief and affect equations, suggesting that exposure to
television contributes to the endogenous variables beyond what could
be expected from X alone. Or, to put the matter another way, X (as
it is understood here) cannot completely account for the relationship
between TVEXP and the endogenous variables.

On the other hand, in no case does ADEXP make a significant
contribution in the presence of TVEXP. Thus it would appear that
the relationship between TVEXP and the endogenous variables may
be largely explained by exposure to television alone.

TABLE 8.6

Coefficients for a Model of TVEXP

Variables	Coefficient	Standard Error	p
Grade	-.163	.0182	<.01
Socioeconomic status	-.132	.0244	<.01
Parent-TVEXP	.385	.0600	<.01
Number of television sets in household	.0737	.0196	<.01
Mother's age	-.0889	.0307	<.01
(Constant)	1.26		
R^2	.262		<.01

Source: Compiled by the authors.

Unfortunately this is about as far as the evidence goes. Whether one develops the hierarchy of effects using ADEXP or TVEXP seems, on the basis of the evidence developed here, to be a matter of preference. It may very well be the case that the apparently superior performance of TVEXP over ADEXP in Table 8.7 may be due solely to the high correlation between the two measures (R = .84) and the slightly greater reliability of the television exposure measure (its coefficient α is .89 versus .73 for medicine commercial exposure measure). The researchers have chosen to pursue the model using ADEXP because it seems to be the more plausible causal variable and was the variable specified in advance. Whether this choice is the most propitious can only be answered by further research.

As for the variable X, the results are intriguing, but not at all definitive. Surely the rather positive results in Table 8.7 using a very arbitrary definition for X suggest that this, too, is an area in which future research could be profitably concentrated.

CONCLUSIONS

The substance of the results of this modeling effort point to the following conclusions.

TABLE 8.7

Analysis of the Contributions to the Explanation of
Endogenous Variables by Classes of Variables
Involving X, TVEXP, and ADEXP

Class	R^2	Increase in R^2	p
Belief			
Parent-belief[a]	.207	.207	<.01
ILLEXP[b]	.213	.006	ns
X[b]	.225	.012	<.05
TVEXP[b]	.248	.023	<.01
ADEXP[b]	.255	.007	ns
Affect			
Belief	.285	.285	<.01
Parent-affect[a]	.313	.028	<.01
ILLEXP[b]	.317	.004	ns
X[b]	.336	.019	<.01
TVEXP[b]	.347	.011	<.05
ADEXP[b]	.350	.005	ns
Intent			
Affect	.421	.447	<.01
Parent-intent[a]	.447	.026	<.01
ILLEXP[b]	.463	.016	<.01
X[b]	.470	.007	ns
TVEXP[b]	.472	.002	ns
ADEXP[b]	.478	.006	ns
Requests			
Intent	.480	.480	<.01
PCMU[b]	.532	.052	<.01
ILLEXP[b]	.540	.008	<.05
X[b]	.547	.007	<.05
TVEXP[b]	.552	.005	ns
ADEXP[b]	.555	.003	ns

[a]This class includes the named variable together with the
moderating variables grade, illness anxiety, and specific mediation.
[b]This class includes the named variable together with the
moderating variables grade, illness anxiety, specific mediation,
and parents as an information source.
Source: Compiled by the authors.

1. There is strong evidence both in the coefficients and the R^2 measures for the validity of the hierarchy of effects in this context.

2. The model governing children's behavior with respect to proprietary medicines is quite complex. The introduction of moderator variables appears to be a necessary step in moving toward a more complete picture of the relationship among all the relevant variables.

3. Increasing exposure to television advertising of proprietary medicines does appear to affect positively children's beliefs about the efficacy of those medicines when they are sick. These effects, however, are small and are overshadowed by ordinary developmental changes associated with aging and parental influences as reflected in their own beliefs about proprietary medicines.

4. Interestingly, exposure to television advertising is not unequivocal in its effects. As children get older, there occurs some process that results in a negative association between advertising and affective feeling about taking proprietary medicines. This process similarly affects intention to take such medicines when sick. Yet, beliefs about the efficacy of proprietary medicines and requests to parents for such medicines are positively stimulated by exposure to advertising.

5. Whether the causal agent influencing the various endogenous variables is exposure to proprietary medicine advertising or simply television exposure alone, or yet another variable arising from the family environment, is not definitively answered here. It does appear to be the case that any model must contain some kind of a television exposure variable. Only future research can decide the relative superiority of the two exposure measures.

REFERENCES

Fishbein, M., and I. Ajzen. 1975. Belief, Attitude, Intent, and Behavior. Reading, Mass.: Addison-Wesley.

Lavidge, R. J., and G. A. Steiner. 1961. "A Model for Predictive Measurement of Advertising Effectiveness." Journal of Marketing 25, 59-62.

Ray, M. L., A. G. Sawyer, M. L. Rothschild, R. M. Heeler, E. C. Strong, and J. B. Reed. 1973. "Marketing Communication and the Hierarchy of Effects." Sage Annual Reviews of Communication Research, vol. 2. Beverly Hills, Calif.: Sage Publications.

9

CONCLUSIONS AND LIMITATIONS

CONCLUSIONS

The conclusions from this study can be summarized as follows: Children are exposed to proprietary medicine commercials despite the fact that such commercials are not directed to them and despite industry self-regulation codes. The average child in the study was exposed to 718 commercials on an annual basis.

Children's beliefs, attitudes, and requests for medicines are affected by the televised advertising of proprietary medicine products. The effect of advertising is to offset slightly a significant overall decline in children's beliefs, attitudes, and requests for proprietary medicines as children grow older. These offsetting effects are significant statistically, although they are not of a substantial magnitude. First-order correlations (controlling for grade) between medicine advertising exposure and beliefs, attitudes, and requests are from .12 to .22. Incrementally explained variance for the medicine advertising exposure variable is from .01 to .03, although advertising works in conjunction with other variables in achieving total explained variance.

The magnitude of effects due to the advertising of proprietary medicines to children is not dissimilar to other advertising research results involving adults. Advertising is obviously a contributory factor in consumption behavior and an explained variance on the order of 2 percent is common. This may, of course, translate into sizable consumer expenditures. Thus children are not unreasonably affected by the advertising of proprietary medicines, although one could make the argument that the effects are considerable given that such medicine advertising was not directed at them in the first place.

130

The relationship between the advertising of proprietary medicines and children's usage of medicines is quite limited, reflecting the dominant pattern of parental control over medicine intake. However, the relationship does reach a higher significance level among seventh graders as these children are allowed to self-administer medicines to a limited extent. However, a more appropriate behavioral outcome in assessing medicine advertising's effects on children is requests and, as discussed, there is a significant (although moderate) relationship between advertising and requests.

Children who are highly anxious about illness show heightened (although still moderate) effects of televised medicine advertising. As such, they can be considered a "vulnerable" subgroup within the total set of children. Analysis among young children, disadvantaged children, and children who are frequently ill fails to indicate any consistent pattern of greater susceptibility to persuasion due to televised medicine advertising.

The extent of parental mediation is found to be somewhat limited as measured by frequency of discussion about illness and medicine. The effect of parental mediation is to lead to more positive child beliefs and attitudes toward proprietary medicines. It may be inferred that such discussions, rather than building critical insight, lead to a greater salience of medicines. It may be that parents find it necessary to provide positive information about medicines in order to encourage intake during illness.

The development of children's beliefs and attitudes toward proprietary medicines seems to occur relatively independently of parental beliefs and attitudes. Analysis within the family shows a lack of parent-child correspondence, suggesting that children develop their attitudes based on independent processing of environmental and experiential stimuli. The study, therefore, supports an independence model of attitude formation rather than a correspondence model, and attributes only limited influence to parents just as the researchers have attributed only limited influence to advertising.

Results suggest the existence of a hierarchy-of-effects model leading to requests as the key behavioral variable. There exists a beliefs-attitude-intent-requests sequence such that each step is predicted mainly from the preceding step.

This study suggests that televised medicine advertising performs only a limited role in the formation of children's beliefs and attitudes toward medicines. In the short run, it produces a modest increase in beliefs and attitudes. In the long run, this increase is overshadowed by a significant decline in children's attitudes and beliefs as a function of age and thus cognitive development and

experience. The study further indicates a lack of relationship between advertising and usage (which is mainly controlled by parents)
and finds no evidence that children abuse proprietary medicines.
Usage levels are moderate and the extent to which parents allow
children to self-administer medicines is relatively low.

LIMITATIONS

Several potential research limitations should be noted. First,
the data for this and previous studies have been based on children's
self-reports. An alternative would be to use parental observations,
especially for behavioral variables such as requests, usage, and
television exposure. However, prevous research by the authors
(Rossiter and Robertson 1975) has indicated that parental reports
are subject to a social desirability bias. Also, parents with more
than one child may have difficulty recalling, if not observing, the
behavior of individual children. Experience has been to trust children's reports unless the children are very young and inarticulate
and unless there are plausible reasons why children should wish to
exaggerate or minimize the behavior attributed to them, which
would not seem to be the case with proprietary medicines.

A second potential limitation concerns the inference of causal
relationships between exposure and "effects" from survey data.
Strictly speaking, a controlled experiment in which one group of
children is exposed to televised proprietary medicine advertising
and another is unexposed would be necessary to allow unequivocal
causal inference. As with television research in general, the problem of finding a matched control group unexposed to pervasive
stimuli such as televised medicine advertising is formidable. Also,
there are obvious ethical problems with any design that would subject children to an increased "dosage" of televised medicine advertising in a controlled, that is, unnatural and potentially powerful,
quasi-clinical, setting.

This type of research is virtually confined to survey methodology, and the best that can be done is to demonstrate covariation,
that is, correlation; try to establish time order, as Milavsky et al.
(1975-76) did with their cumulative measure of medicine advertising
exposure and as the present study and Atkin (1975) did with retro-
spective exposure reports; and try to eliminate plausible alternative
causes, notably by applying statistical controls for "third variables,"
such as age, which relate to both exposure and dispositions. It
seems reasonable to conclude on the basis of these precautions that
children's exposure to televised medicine advertising is a happen-
stance of television viewing and that their slightly enhanced

dispositions toward proprietary medicines are the consequences rather than the causes of this exposure.

Related to the survey methodology limitation is the usual caveat that longitudinal surveys, such as Milavsky et al. employed, are preferable to cross-sectional surveys, such as Atkin and the present study employed, when long-term processes are at issue. Actually, the major need is for a longitudinal comparison of childhood medicine advertising exposure with adult proprietary medicine usage, as this is the real issue that has motivated this and the previous research. However, the cross-sectional data on children and their parents suggest a progressive decline in proprietary medicine dispositions and usage as a function of age, and thus cumulative exposure to medicine advertising, which makes it rather unlikely that a longitudinal study would find a different pattern of results on an intraindividual basis.

A further limitation of this and the previous studies is the failure to employ fully randomized samples. Because of this, the point estimates (means and correlations) cannot be precisely generalized to all children. In the present study, for example, some degree of a nonresponse problem was experienced that may have affected the results. Without further follow-up research, it is impossible to estimate the nature or extent of this source of sampling bias. However, it is noteworthy that the findings for the group most often underrepresented in survey research, that is, children from low parental education or "disadvantaged" households, did not differ from those of other groups in the study, suggesting that any loss at the lower SES end of the sample would not substantially influence the results. Possible underrepresentation of the upper SES end of the sample, for example, through unlisted telephones in the parental interviews, also does not seem too serious in that children from these households are not considered to be an especially "at risk" group. Overall, the major relationships in the study, if not the precise point estimates, should be fairly safely generalizable.

Finally, the use of self-administered questionnaires with children and telephone interviews with parents may have contributed to the lack of parent-child correspondence on medicine attitudes and usage because of some hard to define methodological factor. In this connection it should be recalled (see Chapter 7) that the correspondence model was given the best possible chance to emerge in the factor analysis by using Quartimax factor rotation. It is tempting to conclude that any differences due to methodology would be offset by the similarities conferred by the analysis.

Some virtues of the present study also can be emphasized. By far the most important, it is believed, is the attention to validity and reliability. The researchers feel reasonably confident that the relationship between medicine advertising exposure and children's dispositions toward proprietary medicines has been investigated with thorough content validity (the four primary medicine types), good construct validity (the cognitive, affective, and conative measures of attitude and the addition of requests to parents as a major behaviorally oriented variable given that usage is largely controlled by parents), and known reliability. When correlational results are at issue, as in the present study, it is especially important to provide estimates based on reliable measures. Measurement error can make the difference between correlations that are "merely" statistically significant and correlations indicative of practical significance.

Another asset of the present study is the attempt to assess absolute levels of children's dispositions toward proprietary medicines in conjunction with the correlational results. In particular, the symptom-anchored procedure for measuring dispositions allowed considerable insight as to whether a pattern of "vulnerability" for proprietary medicines was characteristic of all children or of those in special subgroups (the study found that it was not). There has been a tendency in previous studies to emphasize the correlational findings at the expense of "baseline" responses, and this can be misleading. Instances were observed where high correlations were not accompanied by substantial absolute effects (notably among educationally disadvantaged children and among older children who are sometimes allowed to self-administer proprietary medicines) and, conversely, where high absolute effects—the "sheer exposure" phenomenon accompanied by stronger dispositions—were not confirmed by correlational evidence (for young children and frequently ill children). On the other hand, the correspondence of absolute and correlational results in the remaining subgroup (children classified as relatively anxious about illness) indicates that true mediating variables do exist and that the search for such variables in children's media research should continue.

In summary, the present study suggests that, although children's usage of proprietary medicines is firmly controlled by parents, the amount of medicine advertising to which children are exposed does have a modest short-run stimulating effect on their dispositions toward proprietary drugs, especially for the one child in four who may be relatively anxious about contracting the types of illness for which these products are intended. The age-related and thus cumulative exposure-related decline in children's dispositions, however, suggests that the longer term consequence of medicine advertising in the context of children's development and experience is to diminish children's attitudes and behavior toward proprietary medicines. In no instances do the results indicate a pattern of excessive reliance on proprietary drugs that might be carried forward into adulthood.

REFERENCES

Atkin, C. K. 1975. "Effects of Television Advertising on Children: Survey of Pre-Adolescents' Responses to Television Commercials." Report submitted to the Office of Child Development, Department of Health, Education, and Welfare.

Milavsky, J. R., B. Pekowsky, and H. Stipp. 1975-76. "TV Drug Advertising and Proprietary and Illicit Drug Use Among Teenage Boys." Public Opinion Quarterly 39: 457-81.

Rossiter, J. R., and T. S. Robertson. 1975. "Children's Television Viewing: An Examination of Parent-Child Consensus." Sociometry 38 (September): 308-26.

APPENDIX A
PARENT'S QUESTIONNAIRE

This questionnaire was administered by telephone on the week following the children's interviews.

Respondent_____ Telephone Number_____

Child's First Name_____ Boy☐   Girl☐

School_____

Grade_____

"Hello, is this Mrs. _____?" (If not) "When would
you suggest I call back?"

"My name is (_____). I am working on a research
study that is being conducted at the University of Pennsylvania. As
part of our study, your child, (_____) and the rest
of his/her class at (_____), recently answered
some questions about health and nutrition. Now we would like to
get your opinions and ideas about the same things. We will want
information only for _____, and not for any other
children in the family."

Date of interview_____

To begin with, I will read you some statements—mostly about health and medicine. By medicine, I do <u>not</u> mean prescription drugs, but items such as aspirin and cold tablets that you can buy without a prescription. For each of the following statements please tell me whether you "agree," "somewhat agree," "somewhat disagree," or "disagree." In other words, there are four possible answers <u>you</u> can give me to each of these statements. Please pick the one that is <u>closest</u> to the way you feel. To repeat, the choices are "agree," "somewhat agree," "somewhat disagree," or "disagree." Some of these questions may sound the same but please bear with us. Your opinions are all that matter. There are no right or wrong answers.

	<u>Agree</u>	Somewhat <u>Agree</u>	Somewhat <u>Disagree</u>	<u>Disagree</u>
When I have a cold, <u>cold</u> medicine can help me feel better.	1	2	3	4
I worry a lot about <u>getting sick</u>.	1	2	3	4
I hate cats.	1	2	3	4
People take medicines too often.	1	2	3	4
I find out about medicine from <u>my friends</u>.	1	2	3	4
When I have a cough, <u>cough</u> medicine can help me feel better.	1	2	3	4
I worry a lot about getting <u>stomachaches</u>.	1	2	3	4
When I have a <u>cold</u>, I like to take <u>cold medicine</u>.	1	2	3	4
I love it when it rains.	1	2	3	4
I worry a lot about getting <u>headaches</u>.	1	2	3	4
When people feel a little sick, they should take medicine right away.	1	2	3	4
When people are sick, they should always take medicine.	1	2	3	4
I find out about medicine from <u>my pharmacist</u>.	1	2	3	4
I love baseball.	1	2	3	4
I worry a lot about getting <u>colds</u>.	1	2	3	4

140

To help me stay healthy, I like to take vitamins. 1 2 3 4

I find out about medicine from TV commercials. 1 2 3 4

When I have a stomachache, I like to take stomach medicine. 1 2 3 4

I love cats. 1 2 3 4

People should take medicine only if they are very sick. 1 2 3 4

When I have a headache, aspirin can help me feel better. 1 2 3 4

If some of my friends are sick, I am almost sure to get
sick also. 1 2 3 4

I find out about medicine from books. 1 2 3 4

When I have a headache, I like to take aspirin. 1 2 3 4

I hate it when it rains. 1 2 3 4

I worry a lot about getting coughs. 1 2 3 4

Healthy people take medicine regularly. 1 2 3 4

I find out about medicine from the doctor. 1 2 3 4

When I am sick I worry about getting even sicker. 1 2 3 4

When I have a stomachache, stomach medicine can help me
feel better 1 2 3 4

I worry a lot if I don't get enough vitamins. 1 2 3 4

When I have a cough, I like to take cough medicine. 1 2 3 4

Vitamins help me stay healthy. 1 2 3 4

I hate baseball. 1 2 3 4

When I am sick, I worry that it will take a long time to
get better 1 2 3 4

I find out about medicine from TV programs. 1 2 3 4

When I am sick I worry about having to take medicine. 1 2 3 4

141

Now we want to ask you some questions where you should answer "never," "sometimes," "most times," or "always."

Here is the first question. Please answer "never," "sometimes," "most times," or "always."

	Never	Sometimes	Most Times	Always
When _____ has a cold, does he/she ask you for cold medicine?	1	2	3	4
Do you tell your child that he/she has to finish his/her homework before he/she can watch TV?	1	2	3	4
When you have a headache, do you want to take aspirin?	1	2	3	4
Do you tell your child that he/she can't watch some shows because they are only for adults?	1	2	3	4
Does your son/daughter ask you for vitamins to stay healthy?	1	2	3	4
Do you tell your child how many TV shows he/she can watch each day?	1	2	3	4
Do you let your son/daughter take cold medicine without asking you?	1	2	3	4
When _____ has a headache, does he/she ask for aspirin?	1	2	3	4
Do you let your son/daughter take vitamins without asking you?	1	2	3	4
Do you tell your son/daughter how late he/she can stay up to watch TV?	1	2	3	4
When you have a stomachache, do you want to take stomach medicine?	1	2	3	4
Do you let your son/daughter take cough medicine without asking you?	1	2	3	4

142

When you have a <u>cold</u>, do you want to take cold medicine?   1   2   3   4

Do you let your son/daughter take <u>aspirin</u> without asking you?   1   2   3   4

Do you want to take vitamins to help stay healthy?   1   2   3   4

Do you sometimes tell your child to watch a TV show so he/she will learn something?   1   2   3   4

When your child has a <u>cough</u>, does he/she <u>ask</u> you for cough medicine?   1   2   3   4

Do you let your son/daughter take stomach medicine without asking you?   1   2   3   4

When you have a <u>cough</u>, do you want to take cough medicine?   1   2   3   4

When your child has a <u>stomachache</u>, does he/she <u>ask you</u> for stomach medicine?   1   2   3   4

Now we want to ask you some questions about how many times some things happen. Please tell me if the answer is zero times, 1 time, 2 times, 3 times, 4 times, or 5 or more times.

How many times a <u>month</u> does your child get headaches?   0   1   2   3   4   5+

Since September how many times have you taken <u>cough medicine</u>?   0   1   2   3   4   5+

Since school started in September, how many times have you and _____ talked about which medicines work the best?   0   1   2   3   4   5+

Since September how many times have you taken cold medicine?   0   1   2   3   4   5+

How many times a <u>week</u> do you take <u>vitamins</u>?   0   1   2   3   4   5+

How many times a <u>year</u> does your child get <u>colds</u>?   0   1   2   3   4   5+

Since school started in September, how many times have you given him/her cough medicine?   0   1   2   3   4   5+

How many times a <u>month</u> do people get headaches?   0   1   2   3   4   5+

143

How many times a year do people get colds?   0   1   2   3   4   5+

Since school started in September, how many times have you and talked about how to know when he/she is getting sick?   0   1   2   3   4   5+

Since school started in September, how many times have you given your son/daughter aspirin?   0   1   2   3   4   5+

How many times a year does your child get coughs?   0   1   2   3   4   5+

How many times a month do you get headaches?   0   1   2   3   4   5+

Since September how many times have you taken stomach medicine?   0   1   2   3   4   5+

How many times a week do you need to take vitamins?   0   1   2   3   4   5+

Since school started in September, how many times have you and your child talked about medicine commercials that are shown on TV?   0   1   2   3   4   5+

How many times a month do people get stomachaches?   0   1   2   3   4   5+

Since January how many times have you taken aspirin?   0   1   2   3   4   5+

How many times a month does your child get stomachaches?   0   1   2   3   4   5+

Since school started in September, how many times have you and your child talked about what to do when he/she gets sick?   0   1   2   3   4   5+

Since school started in September, how many times have you given your child stomach medicine?   0   1   2   3   4   5+

How many times a week does your child need to take vitamins?   0   1   2   3   4   5+

How many times a year do people get coughs?   0   1   2   3   4   5+

How many times a month do you get stomachaches?   0   1   2   3   4   5+

Since school started in September, how many times have you given your child cold medicine?   0   1   2   3   4   5+

How many times a week do people need to take vitamins?   0   1   2   3   4   5+

Since school started in September, how many times have you and your child talked about when to take medicine?   0   1   2   3   4   5+

144

How many times a year do you get colds? 0 1 2 3 4 5+
How many times a year do you get coughs? 0 1 2 3 4 5+
How many times a week do you give your child vitamins? 0 1 2 3 4 5+

Please tell me whether the following medicines are aspirin, cough medicine, stomach medicine, cold medicine, vitamins, or whether you don't know.

	Aspirin	Cough Medicine	Stomach Medicine	Cold Medicine	Vitamins	Don't Know
Anacin	1	2	3	4	5	6
Flintstones	1	2	3	4	5	6
Bufferin	1	2	3	4	5	6
Contac	1	2	3	4	5	6
Di-Gel	1	2	3	4	5	6
Dristan	1	2	3	4	5	6
Hold	1	2	3	4	5	6
Dettol	1	2	3	4	5	6
Pepto-Bismol	1	2	3	4	5	6
Vick's 44	1	2	3	4	5	6
One-a-Day	1	2	3	4	5	6
Persil	1	2	3	4	5	6

145

Now I would like to ask you what TV programs you, yourself, watch.

I will read you a list of television programs that are on TV once a week. We would like you to tell us how often you, yourself, saw these programs the LAST FOUR TIMES they were on TV. If you happened to see a show twice the LAST FOUR TIMES it was on TV, then you would say twice. If you did not see it at all the LAST FOUR TIMES it was on TV, you would say zero.

We are also interested in knowing if _____ (child's name) watched the TV show with you one or more of the LAST FOUR TIMES these programs were on TV. Let's say that you've watched a particular program two times. If _____ (child's name) watched it with you one or more of those times answer YES. If he/she did not view the show with you at least once then the answer is NO.

	If answer 1, 2, 3, or 4 ask				Did your child watch with you that time/ one of these times?	
					Yes	No
M*A*S*H (9:00, Tuesday night)	0	1	2	3	4	1	2
Charlie's Angels (10:00, Wednesday night)	0	1	2	3	4	1	2
Tarzan (10:00, Saturday morning)	0	1	2	3	4	1	2
Maude (9:00, Monday night)	0	1	2	3	4	1	2
Switch (9:00, Sunday night)	0	1	2	3	4	1	2
Monster Squad (10:30, Saturday morning)	0	1	2	3	4	1	2
Starsky and Hutch (9:00, Saturday night)	0	1	2	3	4	1	2
Bionic Woman (8:00, Wednesday night)	0	1	2	3	4	1	2
Jungle Pete (8:30, Tuesday night)	0	1	2	3	4	1	2
Price Is Right (7:30, Wednesday night)	0	1	2	3	4	1	2
Porky Pig and Friends (7:30, Saturday morning)	0	1	2	3	4	1	2
Mary Tyler Moore (8:00, Saturday night)	0	1	2	3	4	1	2
Busting Loose (8:30, Monday night)	0	1	2	3	4	1	2

146

Program							
Fantastic Journey (8:00, Thursday night)	0	1	2	3	4	1	2
Six Million Dollar Man (8:00, Sunday night)	0	1	2	3	4	1	2
Speed Buggy (10:00, Saturday morning)	0	1	2	3	4	1	2
Welcome Back, Kotter (8:00, Thursday night)	0	1	2	3	4	1	2
Smokey Joe (4:00, Saturday afternoon)	0	1	2	3	4	1	2
Meet the Press (12:30, Sunday afternoon)	0	1	2	3	4	1	2
Land of the Lost (12:00, Saturday afternoon)	0	1	2	3	4	1	2
Tom Wonder (9:30, Saturday morning)	0	1	2	3	4	1	2
Sports Spectacular (4:30, Saturday afternoon)	0	1	2	3	4	1	2
Saturday Evening News (6:30, Saturday night)	0	1	2	3	4	1	2
60 Minutes (7:00, Sunday night)	0	1	2	3	4	1	2
Police Story (10:00, Tuesday night)	0	1	2	3	4	1	2
Pink Panther (8:30, Saturday morning)	0	1	2	3	4	1	2
Sunday Evening News (6:30, Sunday night)	0	1	2	3	4	1	2
Police Woman (9:00, Tuesday night)	0	1	2	3	4	1	2
World of Disney (7:00, Sunday night)	0	1	2	3	4	1	2
Little House on the Prairie (8:00, Monday night)	0	1	2	3	4	1	2
Scooby-Doo (9:00, Saturday morning)	0	1	2	3	4	1	2
Rhoda (8:00, Sunday night)	0	1	2	3	4	1	2
Laverne & Shirley (8:30, Tuesday night)	0	1	2	3	4	1	2
Donny & Marie (8:00, Friday night)	0	1	2	3	4	1	2
Happy Days (8:00, Tuesday night)	0	1	2	3	4	1	2
Jabberjaw (8:30, Saturday morning)	0	1	2	3	4	1	2

I will now read you a list of television programs that are on TV EVERY WEEKDAY, for example, Monday through Friday. We would like you to tell us how often you, yourself, saw these programs the last four times they were on TV. So just keep in mind that the following TV shows are on every weekday.

						Yes	No
Mike Douglas (4:00, afternoons)	0	1	2	3	4	1	2
Spider–Man (5:00, afternoons)	0	1	2	3	4	1	2
Evening News (6:30, nights)	0	1	2	3	4	1	2
Mickey Mouse Club (4:00, afternoons)	0	1	2	3	4	1	2
Bewitched (6:00, nights)	0	1	2	3	4	1	2
Today (7:00, mornings)	0	1	2	3	4	1	2
Mary Hartman, Mary Hartman (11:00, nights)	0	1	2	3	4	1	2
Voyage to the Bottom of the Sea (6:00, nights)	0	1	2	3	4	1	2
Match Game (3:30, afternoons)	0	1	2	3	4	1	2
Good Morning America (7:00, mornings)	0	1	2	3	4	1	2
Tattletales (4:00, afternoons)	0	1	2	3	4	1	2
Morning news (7:00, mornings)	0	1	2	3	4	1	2

Now I would like to read you a list of some medicines and have you tell me which ones you presently have in your home.

	Yes	No
Alka–Seltzer	1	2
Anacin	1	2
Bayer Aspirin	1	2
Bufferin	1	2

	1	2
Contac	1	2
Di-Gel	1	2
Dristan	1	2
Excedrin	1	2
Flintstones Vitamins	1	2
Geritol	1	2
Hold 4 hour Cough Drops	1	2
Ny-Quil	1	2
One-a-Day Vitamins	1	2
Pepto-Bismol	1	2
Pals Childrens Vitamins	1	2
Primatene Mist	1	2
Rolaids	1	2
Robitussan Cough Syrup	1	2
Smith Brothers Cough Drops	1	2
Vick's 44 Cough Syrup	1	2

Now I would like to ask you a few questions about your child's health.

Since school started in September, how many times has your child been to the doctor because he/she was sick? _____

Since school started in September, how many days has your child missed school because he/she was sick? _____

Does your child have any allergies?   1 – yes   2 – no

How many times has your child ever been hospitalized? _____

Does your child have any major physical handicaps?   1 – yes   2 – no

149

Has your child ever been seriously ill—other than such things as chickenpox, measles, and mumps?   1 – yes   2 – no

Has your child ever been seriously injured—other than broken bones?   1 – yes   2 – no

Have you or any other member of your household been hospitalized in the
past 5 years? (except _____)   1 – yes   2 – no

Would you characterize your family's health as:

1 – Excellent   2 – Good   3 – Fair   4 – Poor

These next few questions are just to help us divide our interviews into groups. The results are counted by machine. No one interview is looked at individually.

Please tell me your age. _____

Please tell me whether you are:

1 – Married   3 – Separated
2 – Widowed   4 – Divorced

Are you, yourself, employed outside the home or not?

1 – yes   2 – no

(If YES:) Is that full-time or part-time?

1 – Full time   2 – Part time

(If married:) What is your husband's occupation? (Interviewer: Probe for job title and a brief description of what type of work.)

_____

_____

(If not married:) What is your occupation? (Probe for job title and a brief description of type of work.)

What is the last grade of school that you, yourself, have completed?

1 – Some high school
2 – High school graduate
3 – Some college
4 – College graduate
5 – Some graduate school
6 – Graduate degree

What is the last grade of school that your husband has completed?

1 – Some high school
2 – High school graduate
3 – Some college
4 – College graduate
5 – Some graduate school
6 – Graduate degree

In what religion were you mainly raised?

1 – Catholic
2 – Protestant
3 – Jewish
4 – Other
5 – Atheist, agnostic
6 – Refused

(Interviewer: Remember to thank Respondent for taking the time to talk to you and tell them how much the research team at the University of Pennsylvania appreciates their cooperation.)

151

APPENDIX B
CHILD'S QUESTIONNAIRE

This questionnaire was administered in class and most of the instructions were verbally given by the research team to the children.

Name_____
            First   Last

School _____

Grade _____

Age _____

Boy ☐   Girl ☐

How many times a <u>month</u> do people get <u>headaches</u>?

    0   1   2   3   4   5+

Since school started in September, how many times have you and your parents talked about which medicines work the best?

    0   1   2   3   4   5+

How many times a week do you take <u>vitamins</u>?

    0   1   2   3   4   5+

Since school started in September, how many times have your parents given you <u>cough medicine</u>?

    0   1   2   3   4   5+

How many times a <u>year</u> do people get <u>colds</u>?

    0   1   2   3   4   5+

Since school started in September, how many times have you and your parents talked about how to know when you are getting sick?

    0   1   2   3   4   5+

Since school started in September, how many times have your parents given you <u>aspirin</u>?

    0   1   2   3   4   5+

How many times a <u>month</u> do <u>you</u> get <u>headaches</u>?

    0   1   2   3   4   5+

How many times a week do <u>you</u> need to take <u>vitamins</u>?

    0   1   2   3   4   5+

Since school started in September, how many times have you and your parents talked about medicine commercials that you see on TV?

    0   1   2   3   4   5+

How many times a <u>month</u> do people get <u>stomachaches</u>?

    0   1   2   3   4   5+

Since school started in September, how many times have you and your parents talked about what to do when you get sick?

    0   1   2   3   4   5+

Since school started in September, how many times have your parents given you <u>stomach medicine</u>?

    0   1   2   3   4   5+

How many times a <u>year</u> do people get <u>coughs</u>?

    0   1   2   3   4   5+

How many times a <u>month</u> do <u>you</u> get <u>stomachaches</u>?

    0   1   2   3   4   5+

Since school started in September, how many times have your parents given you <u>cold medicine</u>?

    0   1   2   3   4   5+

How many times a week do people need to take <u>vitamins</u>?

    0   1   2   3   4   5+

Since school started in September, how many times have you and your parents talked about when you should take medicine?

    0   1   2   3   4   5+

How many times a <u>year</u> do <u>you</u> get <u>colds</u>?

    0   1   2   3   4   5+

How many times a <u>year</u> do <u>you</u> get <u>coughs</u>?

    0   1   2   3   4   5+

When I have a <u>cold</u>, I <u>ask</u> my parents for cold medicine.

Never _____   Sometimes _____   Most Times _____   Always _____

Do your parents tell you that you have to finish your homework before you can watch TV?

Never _____   Sometimes _____   Most Times _____   Always _____

When I have a <u>headache</u>, I want to take aspirin.

Never _____   Sometimes _____   Most Times _____   Always _____

Do your parents tell you that you can't watch some TV shows because they are only for <u>adults</u>?

Never _____   Sometimes _____   Most Times _____   Always _____

To help me <u>stay healthy</u>, I <u>ask</u> my parents for vitamins.

Never _____   Sometimes _____   Most Times _____   Always _____

Do your parents tell you how many TV shows you can watch each day?

Never _____   Sometimes _____   Most Times _____   Always _____

Do your parents let you take cold medicine without asking them?

Never_____ Sometimes_____ Most Times_____ Always_____

When I have a headache, I ask my parents for aspirin.

Never_____ Sometimes_____ Most Times_____ Always_____

Do your parents let you take vitamins without asking them?

Never_____ Sometimes_____ Most Times_____ Always_____

Do your parents tell you how late you can stay up to watch TV?

Never_____ Sometimes_____ Most Times_____ Always_____

When I have a stomachache, I want to take stomach medicine.

Never_____ Sometimes_____ Most Times_____ Always_____

Do your parents let you take cough medicine without asking them?

Never_____ Sometimes_____ Most Times_____ Always_____

When I have a <u>cold</u>, I want to take cold medicine.

Never _____   Sometimes _____   Most
Times _____   Always _____

Do your parents let you take <u>aspirin</u> without asking them?

Never _____   Sometimes _____   Most
Times _____   Always _____

I want to take <u>vitamins</u> to help me stay healthy.

Never _____   Sometimes _____   Most
Times _____   Always _____

Do your parents tell you to watch a TV show so that you will learn something?

Never _____   Sometimes _____   Most
Times _____   Always _____

When I have a <u>cough</u>, I <u>ask</u> my parents for cough medicine.

Never _____   Sometimes _____   Most
Times _____   Always _____

Do your parents let you take <u>stomach medicine</u> without asking them?

Never _____   Sometimes _____   Most
Times _____   Always _____

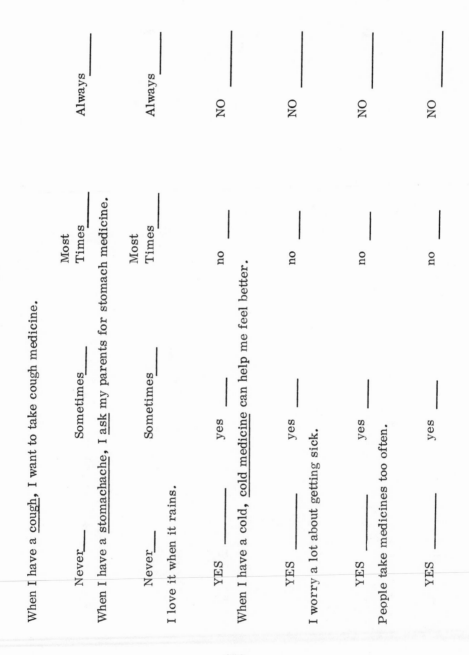

When I have a <u>cough</u>, I want to take cough medicine.

Never ____ Sometimes ____ Most Times ____ Always ____

When I have a <u>stomachache</u>, I <u>ask</u> my parents for stomach medicine.

Never ____ Sometimes ____ Most Times ____ Always ____

I love it when it rains.

YES ____ yes ____ no ____ NO ____

When I have a cold, <u>cold medicine</u> can help me feel better.

YES ____ yes ____ no ____ NO ____

I worry a lot about getting sick.

YES ____ yes ____ no ____ NO ____

People take medicines too often.

YES ____ yes ____ no ____ NO ____

I find out about medicine from my friends.

YES _____   yes _____   no _____   NO _____

When I have a cough, cough medicine can help me feel better.

YES _____   yes _____   no _____   NO _____

When I am sick, I worry about getting even sicker.

YES _____   yes _____   no _____   NO _____

I worry a lot about getting stomachaches.

YES _____   yes _____   no _____   NO _____

I find out about medicine from my teachers.

YES _____   yes _____   no _____   NO _____

When I have a cold, I like to take cold medicine.

YES _____   yes _____   no _____   NO _____

I hate baseball.

YES _____   yes _____   no _____   NO _____

I worry a lot about getting <u>headaches.</u>

YES _____   yes _____   no _____   NO _____

When people feel a little sick, they should take medicine.

YES _____   yes _____   no _____   NO _____

<u>Vitamins</u> help me stay healthy.

YES _____   yes _____   no _____   NO _____

I find out about medicine from the <u>school nurse.</u>

YES _____   yes _____   no _____   NO _____

I love cats.

YES _____   yes _____   no _____   NO _____

To help me stay healthy, I like to take vitamins.

YES _____   yes _____   no _____   NO _____

I find out about medicine from TV commercials.

YES _____   yes _____   no _____   NO _____

When I have a stomachache, I like to take stomach medicine.

YES _____   yes _____   no _____   NO _____

People should take medicine only if they are very sick.

YES _____   yes _____   no _____   NO _____

When I have a headache, aspirin can help me feel better.

YES _____   yes _____   no _____   NO _____

If some kids in class are sick, I am almost sure to get sick also.

YES _____   yes _____   no _____   NO _____

I find out about medicine from books.

YES _____ yes ____ no ____ NO _____

When I have a <u>headache</u>, I like to take <u>aspirin</u>.

YES _____ yes ____ no ____ NO _____

I worry a lot about getting <u>coughs</u>.

YES _____ yes ____ no ____ NO _____

Healthy people take medicine regularly.

YES _____ yes ____ no ____ NO _____

When I am sick, I worry about having to take medicine.

YES _____ yes ____ no ____ NO _____

I find out about medicine from the <u>doctor</u>.

YES _____ yes ____ no ____ NO _____

YES _____ yes ____ no ____ NO _____

I love baseball.

YES _____ yes _____ no _____ NO _____

When I have a stomachache, stomach medicine can help me feel better.

YES _____ yes _____ no _____ NO _____

I worry a lot if I don't get enough vitamins.

YES _____ yes _____ no _____ NO _____

When I have a cough, I like to take cough medicine.

YES _____ yes _____ no _____ NO _____

I hate cats.

YES _____ yes _____ no _____ NO _____

When people are sick, they should always take medicine.

YES _____ yes _____ no _____ NO _____

YES _____ yes _____ no _____ NO _____

I find out about medicine from my parents.

YES _____   yes _____   no _____   NO _____

When I am sick, I worry that it will take a long time to get better.

YES _____   yes _____   no _____   NO _____

I find out about medicine from TV programs.

YES _____   yes _____   no _____   NO _____

I hate it when it rains.

YES _____   yes _____   no _____   NO _____

I worry a lot about getting colds.

YES _____   yes _____   no _____   NO _____

	Aspirin	Cough Medicine	Stomach Medicine	Cold Medicine	Vitamins	Don't Know
Anacin is:	___	___	___	___	___	___
Flintstones is:	___	___	___	___	___	___
Bufferin is:	___	___	___	___	___	___
Contac is:	___	___	___	___	___	___
Di-Gel is:	___	___	___	___	___	___
Dristan is:	___	___	___	___	___	___
Hold is:	___	___	___	___	___	___
Dettol is:	___	___	___	___	___	___

	Aspirin	Cough Medicine	Stomach Medicine	Cold Medicine	Vitamins	Don't Know
Pepto-Bismol is:	___	___	___	___	___	___
Vick's 44 is:	___	___	___	___	___	___
One-a-Day is:	___	___	___	___	___	___
Persil is:	___	___	___	___	___	___

	# Times Viewing					Viewing with Parent
Tarzan (10:00, Saturday morning)	0	1	2	3	4	yes no
Monster Squad (10:30, Saturday morning)	0	1	2	3	4	yes no
Porky Pig and Friends (7:30, Saturday morning)	0	1	2	3	4	yes no
Speed Buggy (10:00, Saturday morning)	0	1	2	3	4	yes no
Tom Wonder (9:30, Saturday morning)	0	1	2	3	4	yes no
Pink Panther (8:30, Saturday morning)	0	1	2	3	4	yes no
Scooby-Doo (9:00, Saturday morning)	0	1	2	3	4	yes no
Jabberjaw (8:30, Saturday morning)	0	1	2	3	4	yes no
Charlie's Angels (10:00, Wednesday night)	0	1	2	3	4	yes no
M*A*S*H (9:00, Tuesday night)	0	1	2	3	4	yes no
Maude (9:00, Monday night)	0	1	2	3	4	yes no

Program							
Switch (9:00, Sunday night)	0	1	2	3	4	yes	no
Starsky and Hutch (9:00, Saturday night)	0	1	2	3	4	yes	no
Bionic Woman (8:00, Wednesday night)	0	1	2	3	4	yes	no
Jungle Pete (8:30, Tuesday night)	0	1	2	3	4	yes	no
Price Is Right (7:30, Wednesday night)	0	1	2	3	4	yes	no
Mary Tyler Moore (8:00, Saturday night)	0	1	2	3	4	yes	no
Busting Loose (8:30, Monday night)	0	1	2	3	4	yes	no
Fantastic Journey (8:00, Thursday night)	0	1	2	3	4	yes	no
Six Million Dollar Man (8:00, Sunday night)	0	1	2	3	4	yes	no
Welcome Back, Kotter (8:00, Thursday night)	0	1	2	3	4	yes	no
Smokey Joe (4:00, Saturday afternoon)	0	1	2	3	4	yes	no
Meet the Press (12:30, Sunday afternoon)	0	1	2	3	4	yes	no
Land of the Lost (12:00, Saturday afternoon)	0	1	2	3	4	yes	no
Sports Spectacular (4:30, Saturday afternoon)	0	1	2	3	4	yes	no
Saturday Evening News (6:30, Saturday night)	0	1	2	3	4	yes	no
60 Minutes (7:00, Sunday night)	0	1	2	3	4	yes	no
Police Story (10:00, Tuesday night)	0	1	2	3	4	yes	no
Sunday Evening News (6:30, Sunday night)	0	1	2	3	4	yes	no
Police Woman (9:00, Tuesday night)	0	1	2	3	4	yes	no
World of Disney (7:00, Sunday night)	0	1	2	3	4	yes	no
Little House on the Prairie (8:00, Monday night)	0	1	2	3	4	yes	no
Rhoda (8:00, Sunday night)	0	1	2	3	4	yes	no
Laverne & Shirley (8:00, Tuesday night)	0	1	2	3	4	yes	no
Donny & Marie (8:00, Friday night)	0	1	2	3	4	yes	no
Happy Days (8:00, Tuesday night)	0	1	2	3	4	yes	no
Mike Douglas (4:00, afternoons)	0	1	2	3	4	yes	no
Spider-Man (5:00, afternoons)	0	1	2	3	4	yes	no

	# Times Viewing					Viewing with Parent	
Evening News (6:30, nights)	0	1	2	3	4	yes	no
Mickey Mouse Club (4:00, afternoons)	0	1	2	3	4	yes	no
Bewitched (6:00, nights)	0	1	2	3	4	yes	no
Today (7:00, mornings)	0	1	2	3	4	yes	no
Mary Hartman, Mary Hartman (11:00, nights)	0	1	2	3	4	yes	no
Voyage to the Bottom of the Sea (6:00, nights)	0	1	2	3	4	yes	no
Match Game (3:30, afternoons)	0	1	2	3	4	yes	no
Good Morning America (7:00, mornings)	0	1	2	3	4	yes	no
Tattletales (4:00, afternoons)	0	1	2	3	4	yes	no
Morning News (7:00, mornings)	0	1	2	3	4	yes	no

My parents allow me to tell them if I think my ideas are better than theirs.	Yes	No
My parents are always getting after me.	Yes	No
My parents enjoy going on drives, trips, or visits with me.	Yes	No
My parents think about me a lot.	Yes	No
My parents let me help decide how to do things we are working on.	Yes	No
My parents forget to get me things I need.	Yes	No
My parents are able to make me feel better when I am upset.	Yes	No
My parents think I am just someone to "put up with."	Yes	No
My parents make me feel good when I am with them.	Yes	No
My parents think my ideas are silly.	Yes	No
My parents enjoy doing things with me.	Yes	No

	Yes	No
My parents try to understand how I feel about things.	Yes	No
My parents almost always complain about what I do.	Yes	No
My parents say that I shouldn't argue with adults.	Yes	No
My parents enjoy working with me in the house or yard.	Yes	No
My parents show me that they love me.	Yes	No
My parents make me feel relaxed when I am with them.	Yes	No
My parents get cross and angry about little things I do.	Yes	No
My parents comfort me when I am afraid.	Yes	No
My parents hardly notice when I am good at home or at school.	Yes	No
My parents are easy to talk to.	Yes	No
My parents act as though I am in the way.	Yes	No
My parents cheer me up when I am sad.	Yes	No
My parents are always telling me I do things wrong	Yes	No
My parents say that I shouldn't talk back to them.	Yes	No
My parents wish I were a different kind of person.	Yes	No
My parents say that my ideas are important and that I should explain them even if people don't like them.	Yes	No
When I ask my parents things, they tell me that "I'll know better when I grow up."	Yes	No

	Names	Ages
Brothers	_____	_____
	_____	_____
	_____	_____
	_____	_____
Sisters	_____	_____
	_____	_____
	_____	_____
	_____	_____

How many television sets do you have in your home that
actually work? _____

Do you have a television set in your room?   Yes   No

Your telephone number is _____

Your dad's name is _____

Your mom's name is _____

INDEX

ABOUT THE AUTHORS

THOMAS S. ROBERTSON is professor and chairperson of the marketing department, The Wharton School, University of Pennsylvania, and director of the Center for Research on Media and Children. He has taught previously at Harvard, UCLA, and Northwestern University. He received his Ph.D. in marketing from Northwestern University concurrently with an M.A. in sociology.

Publications by Dr. Robertson have appeared in many business and behavioral science journals. He is the author of Innovative Behavior and Communication (Holt, Rinehart and Winston, 1971), Consumer Behavior (Scott, Foresman, 1970), coeditor with Harold H. Kassarjian, of Perspectives in Consumer Behavior (Scott, Foresman, 1973), coeditor, with Scott Ward, of Consumer Behavior: Theoretical Sources (Prentice-Hall, 1973), and coauthor of Research on the Effects of Television Advertising on Children (Lexington Books, 1979).

JOHN R. ROSSITER, previously associated with the Center for Research on Media and Children, is an associate professor, Graduate School of Business, Columbia University.

Dr. Rossiter received his Ph.D. in communications from the University of Pennsylvania in 1974. He has an M.S. in marketing from UCLA and an undergraduate honors degree in psychology from the University of Western Australia.

Publications by Dr. Rossiter have appeared in several business journals, including the Journal of Consumer Research and the Journal of Marketing Research. He also has publications in psychology, sociology, and communication research, and is coauthoring a new book on communication models applied to advertising. He is a member of the American Marketing Association, Association for Consumer Research, International Communication Association, and the Australian, British, and American Psychological Associations.

TERRY C. GLEASON is associate professor of marketing at The Wharton School, University of Pennsylvania. Before joining the Wharton faculty, Professor Gleason taught industrial administration at Carnegie-Mellon University.

His specialty is research methodology for the behavioral sciences, particularly applications of multivariate data analysis techniques. Over the course of his career he has taught substantive courses in social psychology, organizational behavior, and marketing, as well as quantitatively oriented courses in multivariate statistics, decision theory, mathematical psychology, and research methodology. His publications have appeared in Psychometrika, Psychological Review, Journal of Personality and Social Psychology, and Journal of Applied Social Psychology.